THE SIX SECRETS OF
RAISING
CAPITAL

THE SIX SECRETS OF
RAISING CAPITAL

AN INSIDER'S GUIDE
FOR ENTREPRENEURS

BILL FISHER

BK

Berrett–Koehler Publishers, Inc.
San Francisco
a BK Business book

Berrett-Koehler Publishers, Inc.
235 Montgomery Street, Suite 650
San Francisco, CA 94104-2916
Tel: (415) 288-0260   Fax: (415) 362-2512   www.bkconnection.com

Ordering Information
Quantity sales. Special discounts are available on quantity purchases by corporations, associations, and others. For details, contact the "Special Sales Department" at the Berrett-Koehler address above.

Individual sales. Berrett-Koehler publications are available through most bookstores. They can also be ordered directly from Berrett-Koehler: Tel: (800) 929-2929; Fax: (802) 864-7626; www.bkconnection.com

Orders for college textbook/course adoption use. Please contact Berrett-Koehler: Tel: (800) 929-2929; Fax: (802) 864-7626.

Orders by U.S. trade bookstores and wholesalers. Please contact Ingram Publisher Services, Tel: (800) 509-4887; Fax: (800) 838-1149; E-mail: customer.service@ ingrampublisherservices.com; or visit www.ingrampublisherservices.com/Ordering for details about electronic ordering.

Berrett-Koehler and the BK logo are registered trademarks of Berrett-Koehler Publishers, Inc.

Printed in the United States of America

Berrett-Koehler books are printed on long-lasting acid-free paper. When it is available, we choose paper that has been manufactured by environmentally responsible processes. These may include using trees grown in sustainable forests, incorporating recycled paper, minimizing chlorine in bleaching, or recycling the energy produced at the paper mill.

Library of Congress Cataloging-in-Publication Data

Fisher, Bill.
   The six secrets of raising capital : an insider's guide for entrepreneurs / Bill Fisher.—First Edition.
      pages cm
   Summary: "The only book on raising startup capital written by a professional who has himself raised over a billion dollars that goes deeper into the standard "how-to" process of raising capital to highlight and reveals those hidden factors that no one but a true insider would know to look for"—Provided by publisher.
   ISBN 978-1-62656-239-4 (paperback)
   1. New business enterprises—Finance.   2. Small business—Finance.   3. Venture capital.   I. Title.
   HG4027.6.F57 2014
   658.15'224—dc23
                                                                      2014019295

First Edition

18 17 16 15 14   10 9 8 7 6 5 4 3 2 1

Cover Design: Steve Pisano

Interior Design: George Whipple

Four miracles in my life—
Will, Lila, Lena, and Michelle

Contents

Introduction

I learned the lessons contained in this book during fifteen years of raising start-up capital for a variety of new businesses, in a number of countries, and I did so largely through trial and error. I completed thousands of investor presentations, hundreds of follow-up meetings, countless scores of due-diligence exercises, many term sheet negotiations, and dozens of successful closings with angel investors, venture capital firms, private equity funds, hedge funds, strategic investors, large commercial banks, and public market offerings. I have compressed fifteen years of capital-raising lessons into the pages of this slender book. If you study this book, you will raise your start-up capital. More importantly, you can then spend your fifteen years learning some other, more contemporary lessons. Thus is progress achieved.

Trial and error was a costly way to learn lessons; however, the advantage is that I ended up rock-certain of what works and what does not. Most of what entrepreneurs are taught in formal academic settings, or receive as advice from well-meaning friends and family, is rubbish. In some ways, it is worse than useless: entrepreneurs with transformational ideas are prevented from entering the business ecosystem: they are coached to knock on the wrong doors, they are taught to speak the wrong language, they are directed to travel the wrong roads. Dogged by their resultant failure to raise any meaningful capital, their spirits eventually flag. They give up, and the transformation that could have been is filed away in that sad folder where dreams go to die—the folder labeled "If Only."

I had the advantage of starting my first business after a successful career as a senior executive with Wells Fargo Bank. As I gained experience as an entrepreneur, I was able to recognize patterns of effective practices, and this allowed me to systematize my methods into an orderly formula. Many of my start-up protégés have followed these steps in successfully raising their own capital, and these methods have proven portable to worldwide markets, with successful capital raises accomplished in the United States, Europe, Australia, and the Middle East.

SECRET 1 Great business ideas do not get funded. Go back and read this phrase again. You will not find this assertion anywhere in the literature of so-called training for entrepreneurs. And yet it is an essential truth for raising capital. Of course, it seems reasonable, looking on from afar, that great business ideas would get funded. And this has led the pooh-bahs of the business world to focus the would-be entrepreneur on a set of mostly distracting tasks. What does get funded? Great business stories. And compelling business stories have a precise set of ingredients and an unvarying order in how those ingredients are organized. These blueprints are revealed in Secret 1.

SECRET 2 No investor will read your business plan. Think about that. Think of the millions of hours business students are frittering away creating long elaborate plans that will go unread. It must be somewhere close, in total wasted pages, to the count of unread novels by would-be authors. There may be value in learning how to construct charming sentences on a sheet of paper, but it is not related to the art of raising capital. There is an essential kit of presentation materials required to persuade an investor to write you a check, and—great news!—not one of them is a business plan. You will discover how to construct this essential kit in Secret 2.

SECRET 3 Money has a personality. What does that mean? It is not enough for you to raise start-up capital. Your capital partner has a distinct personality, most of which is preordained by the patch they have chosen to work within the vast geography of the global capital markets terrain. And personality matters, because your investor does not write you a check and then recede into the night. He or she becomes your long-term partner. What kind of partner is right for you, and who is your best long-term match? Secret 3 can save you not only a lot of time in fruitless matchmaking, but also a great deal of grief in avoiding a bad long-term marriage.

SECRET 4 Dating is your new job. This secret collects the chaotic and emotionally draining events of the capital-raising cycle into an easily learned routine: it's exactly like dating. This dating cycle will not resemble finding and marrying your high school sweetheart. Rather, you will assemble, over time, a network of sweethearts. And you will go on wooing and partnering with and occasionally getting dumped by old and new sweethearts alike, for as long as you are running a business, however large, however small. Your new job is dating.

SECRET 5 Raising capital can cost you your dream. This danger arises because when you persuade a professional investor to partner in your business, you will negotiate the terms of that investment. The investor has negotiated dozens or perhaps even hundreds of investments, and you have likely negotiated none. In effect, you have sat down at the table to participate in a high-stakes poker game, and, unaware of the consequences of your own ignorance, you have invited the professional poker players to teach you the game. They will. Secret 5 will prepare you to negotiate intelligently, to avoid fatal mistakes, and to discover breakthrough compromises on particularly thorny issues.

SECRET 6 The wire closes the deal. In the final flurry of document signing, list ticking, and funds wiring, you will need to adopt the obsessive behavior of a flight controller landing a large passenger airplane during a storm.

Your deal is not closed until the funds are in your business checking account, and until that finality occurs, every unmanaged detail is a danger to the successful conclusion of your months-long journey to raising capital. Secret 6 will present you with a series of simple and time-tested procedures for managing the chaos of a closing without pulling your hair out in the process.

At the end of each secret is a summary of the key points covered. Following that section, I offer a common myth, related to the topic of each secret, which has caused thousands of entrepreneurs to be working down the wrong path.

It is important to note the small number of essential lessons here: there are six secrets, not twenty-seven. Because these lessons grow out of my own first-hand experience, I have chosen to be brutally brief leaving out everything that may be nice but is not strictly necessary. This approach is similar to the difference between a novice backpacker and an experienced one. As a novice, you decide to go backpacking for the first time and step into REI to have the salesman outfit you with everything he says you will need. Then, once you hit the trail, you find out that the load is simply too cumbersome to carry and most of what you brought along is, in the actual event, useless or superfluous. As an experienced backpacker, you travel extremely light and burden yourself only with equipment that is absolutely essential and proven to work. This book travels light.

These six secrets also follow an established order. Using these secrets out of their natural order will not work. It would be like swinging at a tennis ball after it has gone past you. You may have the most perfect tennis stroke of all time, but it does not matter if the ball is not in a position to be struck.

While the six secrets encompass each step of the raising-capital process, there is one essential trait that holds them all together: commitment. Because you cannot learn commitment, no section of this book is dedicated to it. Commitment is a choice that you make. Are you committed to building the business in which you want your investor to invest? If you are not committed, the investor can sense it. You cannot pretend to commit; it cannot be faked. That is why the smartest investors always want to know what capital of your own has been put at risk in order to build your business. This is the closest proxy the investor can get for measuring your commitment. Investors care about your commitment because they know you are embarking on a long journey, full of many surprises and disappointments. There will be times when only your underlying commitment will see you through.

This is not a book of instructions on how to build a successful business. Building a successful long-term business is a complicated, multifaceted achievement, full of random occurrences that require split-second decisions, critical contributions from many people, and a lot of luck. This is simply a book on how to raise capital for your business so you can get onto the playing field. If you are not on the playing field, you cannot win the game.

Whether you follow the advice in this book or not, do not take the advice of those who have never raised their own start-up capital for their own start-up businesses. These well-meaning advisers are amateurs, no matter how talented they are as individuals or how lofty their position in their own field. Rule of thumb: If you want to know how to do something, talk to someone who has already done it, and more than once.

If you learn and apply the lessons in this book, you will gain more than the proficiency needed to raise the start-up capital to get your idea funded and off the ground. After incorporating the lessons learned, you will be prepared to engage in successive rounds of capital raising throughout the life of the business. If you find the idea of raising capital tiresome, you can entirely avoid this phase of business building by choosing to let someone else on your team raise the capital. But be forewarned how that turns out: the person who raises the capital will end up the leader of your business, not you.

Many of the best entrepreneurs are driven by their belief that they can make things better through their idea. They want their work to matter. They do not want to end up feeling like they are simply one of thousands of cogs in a giant corporate wheel, a wheel that would surely go on turning whether they came to work each day or not.

But to turn our ideas into realities, we need to raise start-up capital. Without that life-giving elixir, our ideas never see the light of day. They have no oxygen to breathe, they do not grow up to be anything, and the world will never know what could have been.

There is nothing inevitable about the business future. Steve Jobs and Steve Wozniak did not know that the company they created would one day be a dominant global high-tech brand. Walt Disney did not know, after being turned down by one hundred banks in a row for financing, that his initial theme park would spawn an entire worldwide entertainment industry. Mark Zuckerberg had no idea that his small college experiment would soon be valued as a company worth more than $50 billion. What turned their ideas into a reality, and gave them the chance to become what we now know them to be, was that these entrepreneurs found a way to transform their ideas into fledgling businesses. They raised enough capital to get going.

The next twenty to fifty years of the business future will likewise belong to those entrepreneurs who today, right at this moment, are busy finding a way to get going. Who is to say your idea cannot become a reality? Do you honestly believe that all the other entrepreneurs are smarter or more talented than you are? What is stopping you from becoming one of these entrepreneurs?

Study this book well. Go raise your capital. Make your idea into something real. Take your shot.

—Bill Fisher

Great Business Ideas Do Not Get Funded

Intuit, a $20 billion global high-tech company born and built in the Silicon Valley, was never able to raise a single dollar of venture capital funding, despite seven years of pitching investors. Hotmail, founded by Sabeer Bhatia, and ultimately bought by Microsoft for $450 million, was not able to raise funding, despite desperate attempts to gain interest from angel groups, seed investors, and venture capital firms, until they had already gained traction with hundreds of thousands of users. On the other side of the coin, five out of ten companies that receive venture capital investment fail within three years. Clearly, something else is at work here, beyond the intrinsic merit of the business idea. If great business ideas do not get funded, what is the answer? You can see the outline of this answer in that familiar quote from the famous British economist John Maynard Keynes, that "business decisions . . . can only be taken as a result of animal spirits." What is it that triggers our animal spirits, what moves human emotions? Is it facts? The English novelist E. M. Forster makes a useful observation about the relative value of facts. Here, he says, are the facts: The queen died, and the king died. And here, he says, is the story: The queen died, and the king died of a broken heart. Which phrase touched you just now? Which way of telling gave you a rush of emotion? Humans are motivated, moved, by stories. And notice that the second phrase doesn't ignore or exclude the facts, it incorporates the facts into a story. And there is your answer: Great business stories get funded.

It is likely that, as a businessperson, you do not consider yourself a naturally talented storyteller. It may be the farthest thing from your ambitions or perhaps even a skill you hold in low esteem. But you will not succeed in raising capital and building your business until you become an effective storyteller about your particular idea. This matters. Here is the good news: the craft of composing a great business story can easily be learned, even by those who do not possess the gift of gab. On closer examination you will find that great business stories have a precise set of unvarying elements in their makeup, and a precise order in which these elements appear. If you intend to transform your dream into a reality, you will need to master this composition, which is revealed to you, step by step, in the following pages.

What constitutes a great business story, one that will get funded? Let's dive into the topic. All great business stories are alike in three essential features: (1) they have a compelling story line or plot; (2) the primary actors in that story line are brought to life—made real—through factual substantiation; and (3) the story is memorable.

Let's examine these three features one by one.

There are many effective story-line formats you could choose from, compelling plots that have moved audiences throughout the ages: the hero's exultant return home after conquering some adversity in a faraway land; star-crossed lovers whose blighted future overwhelms their passionate romance; cases of mistaken identity that drive many comedic story structures.

For a business story, far and away the most appropriate structure to adopt is the familiar one of bad guy, good guy, and happy ending. Think of Lex Luthor, Superman, and Superman winning Lois's heart by courageously foiling Luthor's dastardly deeds. Think of PG&E, suspected of poisoning the groundwater near its operations, and Erin Brockovich, in the movie of the same name, tirelessly chipping away at the corners of the terrible truth until she can prove it, and the happy ending when hundreds of affected victims receive millions in compensation as settlement for their claims. Think of Darth Vader in *Star Wars*, and Luke Skywalker triumphing over him and his evil empire, with the happy ending of a universe at peace.

In a business setting, the bad guy does not need to be a human. It could be hunger, or ignorance, or illness, or simple waste. The same can be said for the good guy. It could be food, romance, entertainment, health, or more time and energy made available. When the good guy prevails over the bad guy, that's what leads us to our happy ending.

Let's apply this elemental formula to some successful modern companies.

Who was the bad guy in the Google business story? Lack of access to information: "I know that the answers to my questions are out there somewhere, but I can't find them, and so I remain ignorant." Who was the good guy? Google's search algorithms and technology that collect and make available unprecedented amounts of information to unprecedented numbers of people. And what was the happy ending? Millions of people, performing billions of Google searches and, in the process, participating in the creation of one of the most profitable companies in the history of commerce.

How about online dating innovations like Match.com or eHarmony? Who was the bad guy? Loneliness. Who was the good guy? The technology that enabled millions of the romantically inclined to pair up easily with other like-minded individuals. And the happy ending? Romance, or at least more companionship, and in the process, extremely large, profitable, and fast-growing business models created.

Sounds simplistic, and it is. The essential power of this story line is precisely its simplicity. The existence of entire industries can be usefully examined through this prism. Insurance? The bad guy is catastrophic loss. Banking? The good guy is that your money is safe. Medicine? The happy ending is that you live a fuller life, or at least a life full enough to be able to afford the medical costs associated with a full life. Okay, the analogy only goes so far, but you get the idea. Good guy fights bad guy, and good guy wins, creating a happy ending. In forcing your own business idea to conform to this ancient story form, you strip away all but the essential drivers of your business. You can see clearly what you are building. You can also see whether it is worth building or not. Who is the bad guy your business seeks to conquer? Is it inefficiency, is it some life-threatening health issue, is it a lousy consumer experience in some daily activity? You cannot raise money for a business innovation that does not address a definable bad guy, a distinct problem. And until you can articulate clearly a precise problem your business solves, no one will ever be interested in the solution. A natural outcome of this principle is that, if you cannot clearly articulate a persuasive problem that your business solves, you will not be able to raise capital. It's the very first step in your journey.

If you have, in fact, arrived at a compelling problem that needs solving, then who is your good guy? How does your good guy beat the bad guy, how does your solution solve that particular problem? And, finally, what is the happy ending, particularly a happy financial ending for investors, which will result from your good guy's victory in the marketplace?

I encourage entrepreneurs to think long and hard about these essential story lines in their business idea, and to do so before they invest any time and energy in any other business-building activity. If you don't get this part right, almost nothing else you can do will make any difference to your success. If you do get this right, if you have a compelling bad guy, good guy, and happy ending, you own an inherently exciting business story, and you hold in your hands the most powerful tools of the business-building trade.

We are going to turn next to the second feature of great business stories—substantiating your story line—but I want to pause here to illustrate just how powerful these initial story elements are all by themselves. Here is the illustration: An investor who is captivated by your story will often go out and find the research and the numbers that support the urge to invest in you and your idea. This happens time and time again. In the world of social psychology, this is known as *selective exposure*. After making a decision, we tend to seek out information that supports our decision. We will also avoid information that contrasts with our decision. But the decision is sometimes already made, on the spot, triggered by the investor's animal spirits, which are moved by your adopting an ancient, powerful story line.

Let's examine essential feature 2: bringing the essential story lines in your story to life through factual substantiation.

Great business stories are never works of pure fiction. Investors may be amused or entertained by fiction, but they will not invest in it. If your business story is exciting, if you have an exciting bad guy, and good guy, and happy ending, then the next order of story-building is to substantiate those story lines with illustrations and factual research.

Imagine illustrating the bad guy for an online dating business.

The entrepreneur might put the potential investor in the shoes of someone who is lonely and trying to meet someone to form a relationship. The scenario would show what it is like to go to a public place, such as a bar, spend money on expensive drinks, and watch as the clock nears *last call*. The example would take the investor through this lonely night, possibly during the holidays, with the intention of meeting a quality person but continually coming up short.

The story would illustrate the pain of asking someone out on a date and being rejected. Because the process of meeting someone at a bar is so hit-or-miss, the story would describe the investor walking home alone in the cold. By clearly describing the pain of the situation, you make it real. You can detail the cost of the nice clothes your character buys to wear to upscale nightclubs. You strive to bring the pain to a personal level for the investor. Or put your investor in the shoes of someone who spends $100 on weekly dance lessons in the hope of meeting someone on the dance floor. If the investor can feel your character's plight, he or she will welcome a solution that can ease the pain.

Research and think through the size of the problem: How many lonely souls are trapped in fruitless searches for some romantic companionship? And what is the cost of those searches? Document your research, and name your research sources.

The villain, in your business story, must spring to life, or the investor will not have any interest in the hero. You make your bad guy convincing, you give them flesh and blood, through a balanced mixture of anecdote and researched facts.

After you exemplify the problem, you need to bring the same level of illumination to your good guy. Why will your solution work? Exactly how can a caped, curly-haired man who can fly save the planet?

What are the key drivers of your solution? Breakthrough technology, scale, some innovative service level or marketing innovation? And how do these drivers directly address the problem? The kind of business you are building will dictate the kind of drivers you identify.

For example, one successful business I am familiar with is centered around launderettes. The business partners did a national roll-up of launderettes and recognized two key drivers that would make their solution profitable. First, they discovered that all launderettes used the same supplies, which, individually, they had to purchase at retail prices. However, if you rolled up hundreds of launderettes to purchase supplies, the savings would fall through to the bottom line. So, the first driver was a restructuring of purchasing. The second driver was the recognition that all launderettes lost a significant number of quarters, either through theft or careless handling. Therefore, developing a way of tracking every quarter that was spent at a launderette could be very profitable. The second driver was efficiency. The owner of the business once told me that they were doing about $200 million annually, all in quarters!

There is one other critical substantiation to your good guy, and that is the team of talents you have assembled to execute the business plan. If your key driver is technology innovation, who on your team will be responsible for that innovation, and what is their background or suitability for that role? If the key driver is some marketing analytics, same question. In many respects, you as entrepreneur and the team you assemble compose the good guy in your story.

Most entrepreneurs do not have the resources to hire employees before their funding goes through. If that is the case for you, it is important to point out to your potential investors that you are talking with first-rate potential team members. Explain that you are talking with two or three team members who are qualified to be crucial to your business's success and that you are confident you will get one of them as soon as you have funding.

When explaining exactly how your good guys can win the day, aim to quantify your solution—just as you did with your problem. For instance, getting back to the example of early online dating sites, you might pull from surveys that demonstrate how many single people there are. You could examine how many hours people spend searching for the perfect outfit or working out in order to attract others, or the astounding number of wasted cocktails.

It is extremely helpful if you can give your investor at least a glimpse of Superman flying. Early client interest or proof of early revenue can provide terrific support. Without either, you can still use anecdotal evidence to give a hint of how you will succeed. For example, with the first company I founded, GetSmart.com, my initial investor had seen the prototype of my business, and flying across country on his way out to meet me, he had to stop in three different airports. At each airport he went up to strangers, described my business, and asked them if they would use it. It turned out that every person he approached said "Yes" and asked when the service would be available. Any evidence you have that supports your business is better than saying, "I don't have any clients and I have not made any money." Imagine if you were an entrepreneur of one of the first online dating sites. What kind of anecdotal evidence that supports your business idea could you provide to investors?

And now let's turn to the happy ending to your great business story. For the investor, the only happy ending is that if they invest in your good guy to defeat the bad guy, the business will grow and produce solid profits.

This part of your story will clearly need to be substantiated as well. How does your business make money? Is it monthly subscription, or item purchasing, or dramatically reducing a current run rate of needless expenses? Document your research on this revenue model and provide fact-checked examples. What is the size of your market? When you answer this question, think about how authentic your reasons are for framing that answer. For instance, Tom Proulx, cofounder of Intuit, once told me that in its early stages, his hiring staff asked potential employees how many dentists there were in the United States. The interviewer would ask them to talk out loud to see how they were thinking through and arriving at their answers. Sometimes, the employee candidates would start by recognizing that they had a dentist. Next they would recall that there were about 300 million people in the United States. Once in a while they then arrived to the conclusion that logically there must be about 300 million dentists in the country because everyone needed a dentist. Needless to say, this kind of fuzzy logic never got anybody hired at Intuit.

In describing the happy ending, you will need a realistic assumption of the proportion of the market you believe your business could capture. Again, what important information leads you to this figure? How long will it take you to capture this targeted figure? And what will be the expenses to get there?

Of course, you will need to identify your profit margins. How are you figuring such margins? Are these margins similar to what your competitors are receiving? If they are radically better, what is your radical innovation that will transform your particular industry?

Your potential investors will likely question your budget assumptions. Investors are pessimists, which they became, over time, by backing optimists. By analyzing the information that propels your assumptions, you will be better able to justify to investors why your assumptions are realistic.

Finally your story line of good guy beats bad guy and realizes a happy ending will not be credible in a business setting unless you also address the risks that your good guy faces, one of which is certain to be identifiable competitors. Many first-time entrepreneurs shy away from mentioning the risks in their business, thinking that mentioning these risks will only serve to spook the investor and be counterproductive. This is a misreading of the investor psyche. All investors are nervous, especially when they are in decision-making mode about a potential investment. When you capably point out the risks of your business building, you give these fears a name, which allows you to also talk about how you have structured the business in order to mitigate that risk. Perhaps the risk is that your business will acquire fewer than the targeted number of customers, or at a price-point lower than you have forecast. This allows you to point out that you have answered this risk by, say, locating a professional outside marketing team that has already proven successful in a similar business. Or perhaps the risk is that your innovative technology will not perform as advertised, and you explain that, to mitigate this risk, you have partnered with beta-testing customers who are actively reporting back to you on any potential bugs before the product is released.

You know what worries you most about your own business model, and you have surely taken steps to solve for those worries. Lay it all out for the investor. Far from spooking them, it makes you and your potential happy ending all the more credible.

One important category of risk is the likely competitors to your good guy. There are competitors in any worthwhile business undertaking. If you can find no competitors whatsoever, please stop and rethink your entire business model. It is likely that you are pursuing a mirage. When you identify competitors, mention them as a legitimate risk, and point out your own best reasoning about why you, and not they, are positioned to be more successful.

You have fashioned a compelling plot of a believable bad guy, good guy, and happy ending, and you have made your actors spring to life by factual comprehensive substantiation. Now let's turn, at last, to the third attribute of all great business stories: they are memorable. The secret to making your business story memorable is happily contained in a single word: brevity.

My father was an evangelist who spoke all over the world. He heard a quote somewhere that struck a chord with him, and he repeated it often: "If you want me to give a five-minute speech, I'll need a month to prepare. If you want me to give a twenty-minute speech, I'll need two weeks. If you want me to speak for an hour, I am ready right now." This quote speaks to the price of brevity: it is expensive. If you are going to be persuasive in a couple of minutes, you have to think hard.

"Never was so much owed by so many to so few." Winston Churchill spoke these words about the heroics of the British Royal Air Force during World War II. Innumerable book-length treatments of those same heroics have been penned and published, but his is the quote that is remembered. Why? Because it sums it all up in exactly eleven words. Jack Ramsey was recently asked to define the Twitter business model. He did not launch into a long dissertation on business model dynamics and marketplace forces. He answered: "Twitter moves ideas around." If I asked you to tell me about your business, how long would it take you? Ten minutes? I am not interested. Investors do not have ten minutes. You will never attract investor capital if it takes you ten minutes to tell someone your ideas. If you are like most start-up companies, you have a big vision about how your product or service will impact your community or your world. You have a fuzzy idea about where you would like to be in five years, but no idea how to tell your business's story in a compelling way now—in one bullet of condensed drama. You know that your business has the ability to make big money, but in order to convince someone else, you feel that you need to tell them everything so they'll *get it*.

For most of the business conversations you are going to have as you go about raising capital, and there will be hundreds of them, you will have about 120 seconds to capture your listener's interest. After you pass 120 seconds, you will notice your investor's eyes glazing over, as he begins to think of the groceries he needs to buy, or the golf course she will be playing next weekend. You and your story are already forgotten.

Boil it down: Who is your bad guy, who is your good guy, what is the happy ending? The next secret reveals the formula for how you can reduce your great business story to two minutes. The more concentrated your message, the more likely you are to stand out from the crowd.

CONCLUSION

Great business stories get funded, and they share three essential elements: (1) a compelling plot; (2) factual substantiation of the principal actors in that plot; and (3) brevity. If you can master these three elements, you can raise capital. The secrets outlined in successive secrets in this book will shorten the time frame it will take you to raise that capital, prevent the terms of your capital raising from destroying your dream, and help you discover how to find an investor who will be a great long-term partner. But this initial three-part secret all by itself, when mastered correctly, will provide you the breakthrough to raise capital.

In doing research for this book, I have come to realize that the importance of effective storytelling, far from being some trick of persuasion, is hard-wired into the human psyche. It is inescapable. I ran across this quote by Ursula K. Le Guin, which sums it up nicely:

"The story—from Rumpelstiltskin to *War and Peace*—is one of the basic tools invented by the human mind for the purpose of understanding. There have been great societies that did not use the wheel, but there have been no societies that did not tell stories."

NUMBERS MYTH

For this secret, the biggest myth is that *numbers are enough to attract investors*. People have somehow been led to believe that investing and investment decisions are all a matter of arithmetic. Facts, numbers alone, do not persuade. In order to persuade an investor, entrepreneurs have to be able to tell their stories. The following quote appears in the book *Animal Instincts* by George A. Akerlof and Robert J. Shiller:

> The human mind is built to think in terms of narratives, of sequences of events with an internal logic and dynamic that appear as a unified whole. In turn, much of human motivation comes from living through a story of our lives, a story that we tell ourselves and that creates a framework for motivation. Life could be just "one damn thing after another" if it weren't for such stories. The same is true for confidence in a nation, a company, or an institution. Great leaders are first and foremost creators of stories.

No Investor Will Read Your Business Plan

Investors will not read your business plan for the same reason that book buyers do not first read the book they are interested in buying. What readers "buy," initially, is the title and the look of the cover; then, if interested, they proceed to the blurbs on the back cover, made up of intriguing praise from various luminaries, or perhaps they might research an online review or two. Then, if piqued to further interest, they might read the summary of the book on the flap of the book jacket, or perhaps even dip a toe into the first few paragraphs of the author's writing. Then they make up their minds. If you have purchased this book, it is doubtless the familiar pattern you have followed. But reading the entire book? Of course not. That is an altogether different matter, something that happens much later, or never, as many thousands of books quietly gathering dust on forgotten bookshelves can attest. And even when the book is read, that happens long after the purchase is made.

By the time you are ready to move forward with the second secret, you will have already spent long hours analyzing your risk, detailing your budget, and identifying your competitors. Your team is assembled, or assembling, and their credibility and capabilities are quantified. You understand the problem and know exactly how your solution can solve it. Your story has been written, reworked, practiced, and reworked again. You are able to tell your story up through the happy ending, and people are able to follow along without puzzling looks. Armed with your new compact story that takes people from sadness to joy in one to two minutes, you are ready to steal the breath of potential investors. But not so fast.

In order to sell your story, you need to give it dimensionality with the support of high-impact story materials. There is an essential kit you will need to assemble to demonstrate the kind of preparation investors demand. This kit includes all the materials you will need to get investors' attention. Without it, you will never manage to get in front of seriously interested investors. The essential kit includes the following high-impact materials:

1. Bulletproof Business Speech (one to two minutes)
2. One-page Summary
3. Formal Presentation
4. Three-year Budget (complete with monthly cash flows)
5. Arsenal of Supporting Articles and Research

To understand the importance of this kit, consider the following funnel that you must be prepared to travel through to connect with serious investors. First, you will need to tell your story, on average, 300–500 times to discover or be referred to the people who have the ability to influence your business in positive ways. Next, you will tell your story 100–200 times (more than once to each) to these business influencers to be directed to serious investors for your kind of business. You will then need to work through at least ten of these seriously interested investors to discover the one that is going to write you a check.

As you travel through the funnel en route to securing investment, there will be countless potential dead ends that, if handled poorly, will set you back or knock you from the funnel. Your essential kit will have you prepared for these wrong turns and en-able you to pass by them and advance to the next stage of the funnel.

For example, suppose you tell your bulletproof speech to a group of business execs sitting at the other end of the table at lunch. They invite you up to their office to meet some of their colleagues who might be interested in hearing more about your business. With a prepared PowerPoint presentation, you will be able to captivate a group of businesspeople whose attention you have earned. With a solid one-page summary, you have something you can leave behind to keep your idea in front of them. Without preparation, without your essential kit, you will lose their attention just as quickly as you earned it. The preparation that went into building your story will be overshadowed by your lack of preparation to carry it any further. You will have a room filled with businesspeople who are willing to hear you out, and you will have nothing to offer. That is an awful time to go impromptu. With the opportunity lost, you will need to return to the top of the funnel and start all over again. Avoid wasted time and meetings by focusing now on creating your essential kit.

MATERIAL 1: YOUR BULLETPROOF BUSINESS SPEECH

This is the brief (one to two minute) presentation you build out from the basic story line you created in Secret 1. You will be able to give this speech when you wake up in the middle of the night, when you are on the subway or in an elevator, when you are called upon without warning, or when you bump into someone in a grocery store. It has to go off like an alarm, whenever the opportunity arises. You will tell your story an incredible number of times. The better you tell it and the more compact it is, the more impact it will have.

Looking at your bulletproof speech item-by-item can help you identify any unnecessary bulk that you may be having trouble eliminating. So, whether you are building your speech or refining it, here is a breakdown of exactly what each portion should accomplish in order to make it all-around bulletproof.

The Credibility Builder

When speaking to someone new, you start by establishing a level of credibility. Without this important step, your listener will be staring you in the face trying to understand why you are speaking to them. If you are giving your speech to a stranger, then chances are you have had some conversation leading up to it. During that conversation, you most likely established credibility in a roundabout way that led you to begin your speech. If, on the other hand, you have contacted someone with the intent of presenting, you need to start with linking them to you and your idea. Until you get past the credibility issue, the person you are speaking to will not be listening to what you are saying at all.

For example, imagine that you are launching a company that will revolutionize antivirus software; you have named it *Lockdown Inc.* You could start with, "Hello, I am Bill Fisher, and I was referred to you by Tom Powell, who mentioned to me that you are interested in the development of the antivirus software industry." If you have a name that means something to this person, use it; of course, you will need to have the permission from the person who referred you. If you have not been referred to this person you might start with, "Hello, my name is Bill Fisher, and I read in the *Wall Street Journal* that you have an interest in the advancement of antivirus software." You need to make whatever link you can that allows them to see why you have specifically targeted them with this proposal. You can find additional tips on establishing credibility in Secret 4, in a section entitled "You Get Introduced."

Problem

The next portion of your pitch should revolve around your identified problem: the bad guy. Let your listener know that the problem exists and why it is significant. Let it be known that you are leading the crusade to solve this problem. For example, "I'm leading a senior team that is building a company focused on eliminating the source of most computer viruses, namely e-mail points of entry."

Translate your problem into economic terms: "You probably know that the current industry expense of trying to cure viruses is $20 billion a year, and that number has been growing over 30 percent per year. What is not as well known is that 90 percent of viruses infect the computer purely through the e-mail portal."

Solution

After you have identified the scope of your problem and the pain it inflicts, explain your solution. Allow your listener to clearly see how your solution can correct the problem that you have just detailed. The potential investor should be able to understand why your solution makes sense without needing a PhD in computer engineering. Aim to show the *direct* impact that your solution has on the problem. For instance, "My team has discovered a patentable technology fix for the majority of computer virus attacks worldwide. We've tested Lockdown Inc. software with large-scale beta customers, including Apple and IBM, and it works."

Part of your solution is the expertise of your team. State the experience and skill sets that make your team members credible. For example, "My team of IT specialists is led by the creator of Hotmail. My two software developers were key players in creating the first antivirus programs at McAfee, my marketing team helped popularize Norton Antivirus, and product development is led by a former FBI technology fraud investigator."

Happy Ending

Explain that you have researched your competition, identified your niche, detailed a realistic budget, tested parts of your solution, built prototypes, etc. Show your potential investors that you have not been sitting around with your hand out waiting for money to drop into it.

For example, "So far we've built a prototype solution, tested it fully with large beta customers, and filed for a patent. Our competition is trapped by legacy technology that has them focused on the wrong end of the problem. We believe we can capture 1 percent of that $20 billion market in a five-to-seven-year time frame, creating a company that could be valued in the range of $200–$300 million."

Investor Opportunity

This is the portion of your pitch in which you first mention the available investment opportunity. You might say, for example, "The reason Tom introduced us is that we're going to be choosing an investment partner soon to help finance the scaling up of our marketing efforts." This allows you to draw them back to your source of credibility while you focus them on the investment opportunity.

Competition Identifier

Let your potential investor know that you are speaking with other investors, but you would like to work with them, in particular, for certain reasons. This is the point when you show your knowledge of their firm, if applicable, or of their investment history.

For example, "We are talking seriously with a couple of other firms, but you were suggested by Tom Powell as a potential partner because of your successful history in helping to develop software start-ups."

Call to Action

When you reach this portion of your pitch, you will have already established credibility, identified the problem, provided your solution, outlined the solid progress you have already achieved in building your solution, identified the opportunity for investment, and mentioned why they might be a suitable investor. Now it is time to set up a more in-depth meeting. This is, after all, the point of your bulletproof speech: to get your potential investors to set up a time to hear more. For example, at the closing of your speech you could say, "I'd like to set up a time to explain a bit more about Lockdown Inc. What does your schedule look like in the next couple of weeks?" If you have ended up giving this presentation in a parking lot, an elevator, a subway, a noisy restaurant, you may want to say: "I'd like to set up a time to explain a bit more about Lockdown Inc. I'll call your office tomorrow to find a time that works for your schedule."

Remember, you will most likely give your bulletproof speech hundreds of times in order to narrow the field down, over time, to ten or twenty qualified investors. If you do not put the time and energy into making your speech bulletproof, plan on giving it thousands of times, or possibly for the rest of your life.

MATERIAL 2: YOUR ONE-PAGE SUMMARY

Your one-page summary can be thought of as a physical copy of your bulletproof speech that you can leave with potential investors when it is appropriate. Keep the topic elements, and their respective order, exactly the same. Some parts you may wish to expand on include the background of your team members and a reference to other partners that are involved. Any brief points you can add to legitimize your business idea should be included in your one-page summary. But, as the name indicates, keep it at one, single-spaced page.

MATERIAL 3: YOUR FORMAL PRESENTATION

By now there are a variety of well-known tools for building out your formal presentation: PowerPoint, Prezi, Powtoon, Slide-Rocket. Whatever you choose, keep focused on simply illustrating the powerful story that you created in Secret 1. Great business stories get funded, not flashy graphics. It is your story that is the star.

The most powerful motivator you can offer to investors is to show them how they can benefit from investing in your venture: the happy ending. Build your slides to this conclusion. Your own goal may be to rid the world of evil, but you are talking with a room full of investors, and their view of evil is not being named in the *Forbes*' Richest People list. Keep driving your presentation to what matters to your listener.

Preparing Your Formal Presentation

Your presentation is an illustrated, amplified version of your bulletproof speech. And generally speaking, the presenter who can get the message across with the fewest slides wins. In my experience, you should be able to bring your basic story to life with ten to twelve slides. At the end of this section, I give examples of what each of these slides should cover, and their respective order in the presentation.

Do not plan to read what is on your slides. Your investors can read. Instead, prepare to offer an anecdote, or some commentary for each slide that illustrates or expands the point of that slide.

If you have already assembled team members, plan to bring one or two of them along when you give your presentation to potential investors. This allows the investors to see that there are other clever minds working on your business.

Delivering Your Formal Presentation

Do not move on to the next slide until you are certain there are no more questions on the current slide. The longer your listeners linger on a slide, the better. Of course, there will be times when you are asked a question about something for which you do not have an answer. Do not strain to appear knowledgeable, and never make up an answer in a presentation. Stop; tell the investor that you do not know the specific answer to that question but that you will research it and get back to him. Also, do not expect investors' reactions to mimic their intentions. The investor who watches your presentation but is on her laptop the entire time can give you $1 million just as easily as the one who asks tons of questions and appears to be completely engaged.

Do not hand out any written materials in advance. Giving your audience informational materials up front will have them flipping to the pages that interest them most, and you will have lost control of the presentation. I strongly recommend some kind of projection presentation, and then hand out any written material when you are finished.

In general, you should strive to prepare for your presentations in such a way as to not leave anything to chance. You have presented your bulletproof speech scores of times in order to find someone sufficiently interested and qualified to experience your full story. Make it count.

In terms of thinking through the organization of your presentation, the fewer slides the better; limit yourself to ten to twelve slides maximum length, no matter how complex your business idea. Slide 1 would be the root problem, illustrated. Slide 2 could be the size of the problem. Slide 3 can be the economic impact, or some other vital feature of the problem. Slide 4 will be a clear, unfussy illustration of your solution; slide 5 why or how the solution works; slide 6 substantiation that the solution works; slide 7 the management team of your business; slide 8 a one-page summary of the key financial drivers and financial outcomes of the first three years of operation; slide 9 risks to your business success and how you intend to mitigate those risks; slide 10 an articulation of your competitors in the space. Slide 11 can be a statement of the size of investment you are seeking, by when, and the principal business building blocks that investment will purchase.

MATERIAL 4: YOUR THREE-YEAR BUDGET PROJECTION (COMPLETE WITH MONTHLY CASH FLOWS)

Because yours is a new business, and most likely one that does not precisely replicate any other known model, investors will be driven to verify all of your assumptions. As they go about checking, they will be forming a number of important opinions about you, the entrepreneur: the depth of your own expertise in the field, how your assumptions compare to other somewhat similar businesses and what that says about how well you do your homework, your own personal business common sense, and your intelligence about the necessary financial return that your business, if successful, is likely to give to an investor. All of this makes your budget ingredients extremely important to your prospects of gaining an individual investor's confidence.

Expect everything to be questioned about your revenue line. For starters, be prepared to answer the following questions: Who are the customers, what indications do you have that those particular customers will buy your product, how does the price-point for your product compare to other in-market solutions, how big is the market and how much of the market can you reasonably be expected to capture, and in what time frame, and so forth.

Your homework on these assumptions built into your economic model needs to be spotless. Document data from the best available sources, research comparisons from the best-known examples, and find strong arguments explaining why your projections vary, if they do, from the research or competitor data. And, if the research illustrates a range of outcomes, err on the side of choosing the conservative end of the range.

The expense line will receive similar scrutiny, but the investor will only be interested in expense considerations *if* the revenue assumptions check out. If there are not sufficient revenues to make this an interesting business, it hardly matters what your expenses are. On the expense side, expect scrutiny of staff head count, average salaries, and any sales, marketing, or product development expenses. Be as thorough in substantiating your expense assumptions as you are with revenues.

When you subtract expenses from revenue projections, if your company is forecast to achieve far above the average profit margins for your industry, then you must point to the breakthrough, never-before-experienced factor in your business that will cause that to happen. This could be some technological innovation that abolishes the typical cost structure or some novel economic model that generates unusually high returns. It should not proceed from your belief in miracles.

Your budget forecast is not complete until you prepare sensitivity studies (e.g., pessimistic scenarios that show the effect of, say, your revenues coming in at much lower than forecast rates or perhaps your expenses coming in at much higher rates than you assumed). You are allowed to also present an optimistic case, but only if there is a solid, supportable rationale for believing that the business may grow much faster than your base-case projection.

Be realistic in forecasting your company's growth at achievable rates over three to five years. In achieving that long-term growth you should also forecast the likely size and timing of each succeeding round of financing, and the rationale for each round— new products, scaling up distribution, entering new markets. If this is an early round of financing for your business, do not make the mistake of forecasting that you will never need any more capital. One early round of financing and then long-term success never happens, and your investors know this.

Finally, you must translate for the investor the earnings projections into a likely long-term company valuation, typically expressed as a multiple of earnings. For high-growth new-economy businesses that do not turn a profit, you might need a multiple of sheer revenues. (If you can persuade someone to value your business as a multiple of users, or some other precious calculation that does not include any revenue, I believe you should check your pulse, because you have already died and gone to heaven.) From this projected company valuation, you can then calculate what the current valuation of your company should be in order to give the investor, from today's share price forward, a targeted rate of return of, say, 25 percent IRR. Do not wait for the investor to come up with this calculation. Work with your CFO, or an experienced accountant or banker, to illustrate mathematically why your company deserves a high valuation in this round of investment. The only reason that is persuasive to your investors is that the company will grow to be so much more valuable in the next three to five years that they will realize a strong return on their invested cash.

The valuation that your business should receive today proceeds directly from your financial projections and the future profits you are aiming for. You can support the estimation of the value of those profits by offering comparisons of other, similar companies that have already gone public or been sold, and the multiple of profits they received from the market when they had matured.

As you will learn in Secret 5, the demonstrated facts embedded in your budget should allow you to negotiate strongly for a higher valuation. And your ability to negotiate this early valuation will define a large part of your ultimate financial return from the business you are building.

One further note about your budget forecasts: Be prepared to reforecast often as you get more market data and experience. Because your business is new, it is unpredictable, and so your new company's results will not match your projections; it may do better, it may do worse, but it will not match the expectations. This is extremely frustrating but fundamental to new-business building: the only way to precisely forecast all the expense and revenue elements of your new business is if all the marketplace experience of your new business has already been proven. If everything about your new business is already known, it is not new. In that case, as you well know, you should probably think about building a different business.

MATERIAL 5: YOUR ARSENAL OF SUPPORTING ARTICLES AND RESEARCH

These independent articles help to highlight the essential elements in your story line—the bad guy, the good guy, and the happy ending. Your articles should be timely, accurate, and from credible sources. Find articles that are published by entities that will mean something to your investors. Whereas Reuters, Harvard Business School, and the *Wall Street Journal* would be examples of quality sources; Wikipedia, ToddtheBlogger.com, and NorthernIdaho -Propaganda.com would not. You are trying to build your business credibility through a collection of unbiased articles and research, and so it will be counterproductive to use articles written by sources that have less credibility than you do.

Find three to four credible articles that help to support the need for your business idea. No matter how novel your idea may be, you should be able to find published articles that help to substantiate the value of your business idea. If you cannot find a single article, you might need to rethink your business. Look for articles that identify market trends that show a need for your business. Having a small arsenal of these articles at your disposal gives you the chance to show unbiased research to your potential investors.

As part of your arsenal of supporting articles and research, you should also include a confidentiality agreement. Seek out a qualified attorney to produce a clear confidentiality agreement that will protect the ownership of your ideas. Your investor may balk at signing the confidentiality agreement, but it is standard operating procedure, and not asking is an indication that you are not entirely serious about your ideas.

CONCLUSION

Your essential kit of high-impact materials arms you with everything you will need to take your investors from indifferent to interested. The materials in this kit and an understanding of how to use them are an entrepreneur's ammunition. Not only do they show the amount of preparation you have put into your idea, but also they help answer the questions that investors find most important. In your preparation, you will be forced to crystallize your own ideas and confront hard, sometimes unpleasant facts that need to be included in your thinking. These materials help to build your credibility and will lead you to the investors that have the ability to help launch your business idea.

BUSINESS PLAN MYTH

Thousands of would-be entrepreneurs have been taught that writing a long and polished business plan is necessary to raise investment capital. This is absolutely wrong. While writing a business plan may help you think through some of the more complex aspects of your business, no potential investor will ever read it. Business schools teach their students to write business plans because it can be broken down to a list of steps that are easy to teach, test, and grade. In academia, writing and publishing papers is how success is usually defined. By writing a business plan, entrepreneurs *can* identify potential holes in their business idea, but a lengthy business plan will not be of any real value to investors.

Money Has a Personality

In the entrepreneur's ideal world, they would have one meeting and secure funding. Unfortunately, the world does not revolve around the wishes of entrepreneurs. You will likely endure scores of meetings before you are connected with an investor who has any interest in owning a piece of your business. Even though the *one-meeting-and-done* model is a pipe dream, you can greatly increase your probability of early funding by pinpointing the right type of investor before you begin networking.

When you reach this point of the process, you will have polished your bulletproof speech, you can tell it in one to two minutes on command, and you have an essential kit of high-impact materials. Now, before you start knocking on doors and telling your story, you need to determine which doors are most likely to welcome your knock. You need to take the time to research different investor classes to decide which group will have the most interest in funding your business idea and can be your best long-term partner.

THE INVESTOR UNIVERSE

Because there is big money at stake in the world of investing, an astonishing variety of groups have segmented the market in order to target specific niches. While a huge number of investment groups provide capital to businesses, some of them—such as mezzanine funds, private equity, banks, and public markets—rarely are accessible to start-up ventures. These sources typically invest only in later-stage, profitable enterprises, with predictable earnings flow. Because our goal is to conduct as few meetings as possible, we ignore these institutional classes for the moment and focus our attention on the most likely sources of capital for the early-stage entrepreneur to pursue.

APPROPRIATE INVESTOR GROUPS FOR START-UPS

In order to increase the probability that a small number of meetings will lead you to good long-term partners, spend your time researching and networking with appropriate investor groups. While you are understandably anxious to begin presenting to investors, a week or two devoted to a disciplined analysis of your primary investor market will save you a great deal of time and heartache in the overall process.

Individual Angel Investors

An angel investor is a special type of investor who provides capital support to entrepreneurs. They are special because, unlike other investor classes, they are not acting as part of a formal investment firm. They are individuals who are usually found among the entrepreneur's business or social circle. These are the people you are bumping into every day in your business life. They are lawyers, accountants, bankers, and other businesspeople who have professional experience in business and sufficient personal wealth to be able to make small opportunistic investments. Because they are investing out of their own personal finances, angel investors are generally committing no more than $10,000 to $25,000 to any one company. For an entrepreneur seeking $100,000 in order to begin operations, there will likely be an early seed round of funding that includes multiple angel investors.

While angel investors represent relatively small individual investments, they offer distinct advantages in the early beginnings of company formation. There is the advantage that there are literally millions of angel investors around the world, and a large number within the entrepreneur's personal network, even if those investing activities have been heretofore invisible to the entrepreneur. The negotiation of terms with this investor class is also extremely relaxed. The angel investor generally wants only to be certain of getting in at a price that reflects the early, pre-operations stage of the business, and to be certain that you, the entrepreneur, are personally going to give your best effort in building a valuable company. Perhaps most importantly, the risk tolerance of angel investors is famously high: so high that among angel investors, these early seed rounds are often referred to as "passing the hat," or alternatively, "spray and pray." The important key for the new entrepreneur is to identify those individuals within your business or social circle that have confidence in you personally, or that have a deep understanding of the industry that your start-up business will be targeting.

In addition to offering their capital, individual investors can provide a wealth of valuable industry knowledge and contacts. An angel investor who has invested in similar start-ups in the past may be able to identify known obstacles, make helpful introductions to potential partners, and/or recruit key team members. Linking with an established investor can also help to boost an emerging business's marketplace visibility.

When I was launching my first company, GetSmart, we were able to attract an angel investment from the cofounder of Intuit, a company that had already proven to be a success in financial-services technology. This was an ideal relationship because GetSmart was launching as a financial-services technology company. We also benefited by an angel investment from a former CEO of

MasterCard, which gained the company credibility because GetSmart's first product was a credit-card marketplace. Both of these individual angel investors were a good fit for GetSmart because they brought experience and credibility.

Individual angel investors may be right for you and your business if:

- Your business has high risk: For example, you are mostly at the idea stage, without customers, a proven product, major partnerships, and perhaps few if any team members to rely on.
- Your business needs between $100,000 and $250,000 to launch.
- You can identify a number of business-savvy individuals within your own social or business network who have confidence in you or who have a deep understanding of the industry your business is targeting.

What you can expect from the process:

When working with individual angel investors, it is common to have a single conversation with them, perhaps your bulletproof speech, send them your PowerPoint presentation if they ask for it, and then open a discussion about whether they would be comfortable coming in as one of your angel investors. If they would, you will have prepackaged investment documents, prepared by your law firm, which they will sign, typically without negotiation. Given that the individual investment sizes are relatively small, the investor understands, and you should understand as well, that long, drawn-out negotiations or due diligence processes are unwarranted.

Angel Groups

Angel groups are simply a number of individual angel investors who have found it worthwhile to act as a loose-knit organization of individuals. There is typically little corporate structure to angel groups; you could think of it as an investing club that meets every so often to share tips and consider new investments. While there are formal angel-investing groups, they are far less common than informal angel groups.

Many credit the start of angel-group investing, as we know it today, to Ron Conway and Bob Bozeman, formerly of Angel Investors LP. Conway started the investment group in Silicon Valley in the late 1990s, right in the midst of the dot-com boom. Conway soon brought on Bozeman when start-up businesses were bombarding Angel Investors with plans that needed funding. Conway was a gut-instinct kind of investor who some say would throw hundreds of thousands of dollars at anything that moved. Bozeman came from a technical business background and acted as an inspector to determine which start-ups were truly worthy of funding.

Angel groups today typically provide capital in the range of $100,000 to $2 million. Whereas individual investors may be ready and willing to invest their capital in a matter of days, angel groups usually take between two and four weeks. The negotiation style with angel groups is relaxed but will be guided by generally accepted market terms. Like individual investors, angel groups can carry a high tolerance for risk. Most angel groups meet only a handful of times per year and invite entrepreneurs to present their pitches. After the entrepreneurs leave, the angel investors conduct an internal group discussion about which company, if any, sparked investment interest.

Only a few marketplaces have formal angel groups, but *all* marketplaces have informal angel groups. These informal groups are made up of investors who are connected by some common denominator. Some form informally because a group of people went to business school together and have similar investment interests. Others form because the individuals worked together in the past and had success in a formal setting. Some groups are made up of relatives. Whatever the connection is, these groups can be found throughout the world. However, since they are informal (read: *invisible*), finding these groups and gaining access to their resources can be challenging.

Exploring your own network of business associates and following leads to other contacts can usually help to identify informal angel groups. Established entrepreneurs may know them. Also, many attorneys, tax professionals, accountants, and bankers will have contacts who are part of an informal angel group. Seek referrals from these business professionals, especially the ones who have a business reason to be connected with new ventures.

A formal or an informal angel group may be right for you and your business if:

- Your business has high risk: For example, you are mostly at the idea stage, without customers, a proven product, major partnerships, and perhaps few if any team members to rely on.
- Your business needs between $250,000 and $2 million to launch.
- You can identify a formal or an informal angel group by networking among business-savvy individuals within your own social or business network who have confidence in you or who have a deep understanding of the industry your business is targeting.
- You are willing to trade some additional time for the process to play out in exchange for the opportunity of larger investments than an individual angel investor could offer.

What you can expect from the process:

When working with an angel group, either formal or informal, you will most likely be invited to one of their presentation nights. The group members will watch your presentation and ask more questions if they are interested. Following the presentation night, one of the group members will contact you to express interest or to thank you for your time and inform you that they are not interested. If you do get the call that the group is interested in moving forward, the closing will most likely happen very quickly. It could be as relaxed as sending over the investment documents, getting signatures, and taking the necessary negotiation steps to close the deal.

Crowd Funding

As of this writing, there is a small but growing phenomenon of angel investing that is occurring online, through a variety of so-called crowd-funding sites. Companies like Indiegogo, Kickstarter, and Fundable have created Internet-based platforms for passively introducing promising entrepreneurs to interested angel investors. As with most new entrants to a large powerful market, the early track record of these innovations has been spotty. Entrepreneurs have little or no intellectual property protection, as the sites require posting online the intimate details of one's business plan, which can then be easily copied. The amount of money raised is typically quite small. And the size of the investing audience is limited by existing definitions of qualified investors; in fact, much of the future growth of this nascent channel, at least in the United States, depends on the uncertain implementation of the JOBS act. Partly as a result of these limitations, the early read of the traditional venture markets has been that crowd-funding is a kind of market for lemons: those who cannot qualify for funding through more institutional channels choose crowd-funding as a last resort. Time will tell if this innovation becomes a durable option for entrepreneurs.

Venture Funds

Venture funds manage the money of investors who want to own shares in start-up companies. The venture fund finds the opportunities, vets the investment opportunity, negotiates the terms of the investment, and manages the investment through to realization, returning 70–80 percent of the resulting profit to their own investors.

Unlike angel groups, venture funds seek to invest large sums of money into businesses with high-growth potential. In exchange for their larger amounts of invested capital, usually between $1 million and $10 million, venture funds expect to have a much greater say in the operation of the business than an angel investor. Venture funds are more tolerant of risk than many other investor classes. However, on the risk scale the majority of venture funds would still be classified as distinctly more risk averse than angel investors.

Venture funds expect to see that your concept has been thoroughly researched and budgeted and is outfitted with a core management team. Venture funds will often expect to see proof of existing customers, existing revenues, and major partnerships—or at least some demonstrated traction in gaining these three elements. Venture groups will typically expect a return of capital and a successful exit from the business venture in three to five years, usually by a trade sale of the business or, more rarely, taking the company public. Venture funds are extremely practiced at negotiating all the many elements of a typical venture financing, with a myriad of economic and control considerations that will be mostly unfamiliar to the entrepreneur. In Secret 5 you will learn how to negotiate these terms. But you will never be as practiced as the venture capitalist, and so you are at a natural disadvantage in these negotiations.

Because they seek to invest in companies that are more developed, venture funds take longer to examine a company; from initial meeting to funded transaction, this will generally average two to three months. In the 1970s and 1980s, when venture firms first began forming in the Silicon Valley, venture capital firms were led by successful entrepreneurs who believed their own experience in building companies could be decisive in choosing and then helping to build new ideas with other entrepreneurs. Many of these early venture funds became so successful that their firms expanded and, in the course of doing so, brought in-house the functions of finance and accounting, legal, human resources, and so forth. Over time, as the pioneer entrepreneurial class has retired, these staff members have stepped into their senior roles. Today many of the more seasoned venture capital firms are populated by staff professionals with little business-operating background. This evolutionary turn has not proven to have a bright future, as overall returns in the venture industry have been uninspiring. Inevitably, the pendulum has begun to swing back, and genuine entrepreneurial credentials and operating expertise are once again becoming more common to the backgrounds of many venture partners.

It can be to the entrepreneur's advantage that venture firms are often intensely competitive with one another. Often this is simply the desire to beat the other guy to capturing a piece of the next big idea. There are also firms that have developed a dislike for one another from prior dealings, and of course from time to time senior partners will change firms, which triggers additional competition. While it is always fun to be pursued by multiple bidders, still, in the early-financing stages of a business, I strongly advise you not to choose simply on the basis of who is offering the best terms. Certainly you should take advantage of the market enthusiasm in order to improve your negotiation leverage with all the interested parties, but choose the partner you feel most comfortable with. You are going to be spending a lot of time with this financing partner as you go about building your business. Whatever the perceived economic benefit of the best offer, it will never be worth signing up for a long-term uncomfortable or, much less, adversarial relationship.

Venture fund capital may be right for you and your business if:

- You are beyond the pure idea stage of your business, and you have a product, however fledgling, some early customers or at least verifiable customer experience, the beginnings of a management team, perhaps some strong partnerships signed or under way, and a detailed budget forecast that demonstrates credibly how an investment in your business could produce a sizable return within three to five years.
- Your business financing needs are in the realm of $1 million to $10 million.
- You can afford to wait out the two-to-three-month time frame necessary to find, educate, and negotiate terms with a venture firm.

What you can expect from the process:

When working with venture funds, you will first meet with a venture partner. Then, if that person has reason to be interested, he or she will call for a meeting with the other partners, where you will present, most likely using your PowerPoint presentation. If that goes well, a junior partner will be assigned to your business to lead all the necessary due diligence, and they will be reporting back and forth to the partner who is responsible for choosing whether to recommend an investment. If the partner becomes convinced, he or she will then gain the acceptance of the firm's investment committee, and then the negotiation of terms will begin.

Strategic Investors

Unlike other classes of early-stage investors, strategic investors do not make their decisions based primarily on the potential economic return on investment. Instead, they are looking for companies whose innovation may be able, over time, to augment their own existing business model. Most often the strategic investor is a large, stable corporation, one that needs to be constantly updating its business model in order to change with the times. This corporation finds it more efficient to invest in outside innovation rather than depending exclusively on its own internal creativity. Because of this dynamic, strategic investors can offer the entrepreneur unusually favorable investment terms and are able to invest across the entire spectrum of investment size, from $1 million to hundreds of millions.

With GetSmart.com, the business manager of a leading national business magazine, part of a dominant global media company, decided to invest because he wanted to move the print magazine into the online space. He believed that the experience he would gain by helping to build GetSmart would expose him to new ways of looking at his own business model. The terms of the investment were favorable to our company, and the brand partnership, between our tiny company and this national powerhouse, gave GetSmart.com a tremendous boost in credibility.

Another early strategic investor of mine was the leading provider of worldwide market data. As their entire business model was based on collecting and publishing financial data, this company recognized that the emergence of growing traffic online would offer new ways of accessing marketable data. Again, what led them to invest was their belief that, in helping to build GetSmart, the lessons they would learn could be profitably applied to their own large public business. The deal terms for their investment were favorable, as was the vote of confidence from a respected worldwide provider of market data.

The price that you will pay, as an entrepreneur, for the advantages of a strategic investor are in time and uncertainty. First, because these are large, well-established companies, with busy executives focused on running their own profitable businesses, it can prove very time-consuming to get the attention of the appropriate executive. Second, even when you find the right executive and stir up excitement about the partnership, the decision-making process can stretch out over many months and become bogged down. If you can find a direct senior introduction into the company from someone you know and they trust, and if in that initial meeting there is strong sponsorship potential offered by that senior executive, I would recommend pursuing this alternative. Otherwise, you may be better served by focusing on investors who spend all of their time looking for and making early-stage company investments.

Strategic investors may be right for you and your company if:

- Your business is offering an innovation that could significantly alter or improve the standing of large corporations already operating in related fields.
- You value favorable investment terms above and beyond almost all other considerations, including time and clarity of decision making.
- You can engineer an introduction to a senior executive of a likely strategic investor and find the initial meeting to be strongly favorable to getting a deal done.

What you can expect from the process:

When working with strategic investors, you will typically first meet with an executive who has a strategic reason to be interested in your company's innovation. If she is interested, she will then assign the due diligence to someone in charge of the company's strategic investments, and this person will likely follow the same steps in working up the deal as you would find in a typical venture firm. However, even if the due diligence proves convincing to the investment officer, the internal approvals of investing in your company may hinge on a variety of considerations completely outside your control, such as the political standing of the executive in charge, the overall strategic concerns of the corporation at the moment when your opportunity is under consideration, or even sudden corporate crises that take priority over the making of strategic investments. When and if the decision to invest is made, you will then negotiate terms with the executive in charge of the business unit that finds your innovation strategic.

Hedge Funds

Of the investor classes we have thus far surveyed, hedge funds stand alone in regard to their interest in building successful operating companies. They are not in the business of building successful operating companies; they are traders. Hedge funds, as a broad description, are in the business of finding pockets of hidden arbitrage in large markets and then taking positions—bets for or against certain outcomes—in those markets. They may have research that suggests the value of the Canadian dollar is going to go up, and so they invest heavily in Canadian dollars. Or they may have research that predicts the value of the Indian rupee is going to go down, and so they invest in a market instrument that pays them if the Indian rupee does in fact fall. They may even have research showing that when the value of the Canadian dollar goes up, the value of the Indian rupee goes down, as a result of some obscure but tantalizing correlation, and so they bet on both outcomes simultaneously. As you can see, no companies are being built in these scenarios, although a great deal of money may be changing hands.

The hedge fund investor can be of interest to the entrepreneur, however, in those instances when the company you are building has potential trading applications. In one of the companies I led, we were building a national commercial-mortgage-lending business that was selling, as part of a complex business model, risk-rated portions of the resulting loan pools. While the business we were building was aiming to become a household brand to the small commercial-mortgage borrower, to the hedge funds our business was interesting because they already were trading in those same types of risk-rated portions of loan pools. They found this ancillary product of ours to be intriguing, the same way a wholesale grocery chain, accustomed to buying and selling hot-house tomatoes, might find the idea of buying and selling a new kind of heirloom tomato intriguing. Two separate hedge funds, both of which were already active in underwriting and then trading commercial mortgage loans, came into our business as major financing partners. They secured their trading investment with tangible mortgage assets and leveraged what they believed was their core strength: a deep understanding of the commercial real estate markets. In order to gain an exclusive right to trade our mortgage assets, in a general class of assets that was then in short supply, these hedge funds were willing to invest unsecured equity capital into our operating business, and on terms that were favorable to our company. Much like the strategic investors mentioned in the foregoing section, the hedge fund investors, because they are investing for reasons other than pure economic return from the business itself, can offer the entrepreneur advantages in terms of an equity investment. In addition, because hedge funds see your business from the perspective of its trading applications, the hedge fund can give you valuable insights on potential extensions of your own business model.

The price you will pay, as an entrepreneur, for these benefits, is in experiencing an extremely low success rate in securing interest from a hedge fund. First, your business needs to have a bona-fide trading application in a large market. Then you need to find the hedge funds that are active in that market. And then you need to convince the hedge fund of the value of your company to their trading business. What you will not spend is any significant time with any one potential investor. Hedge funds, unlike the other classes of investors we have described, are making hundreds, perhaps thousands, of investment decisions each year, and as a result, when you get to the right person to talk to, he will not waste his or your time in long due-diligence exercises. Basically it will make sense to him, on the general surface of the idea, or it won't. In my experience, you will usually know within the first fifteen minutes of talking to a hedge fund professional if there is any interest— which blinding speed is, in and of itself, refreshing. Because of the high-pressure, high-velocity nature of the hedge fund business, the industry has attracted some notably mercurial personalities. While it is a luxury to have an investor class that will decide to invest in your company in the space of only one thirty-minute conversation, as once happened to me, the hedge fund investor can also become sour on the investment in about the same space of time. They are paid to be quick to judgment, which cuts both ways.

Hedge fund investors may be right for you and your business if:

- You are involved in a business that has a direct application to trading of particular assets in large markets.
- You can gain introductions to hedge fund executives who are actively trading in the assets.
- You value favorable deal terms more highly than experiencing a relatively high success rate in securing investor interest.
- You are willing to shoulder the necessities of managing a mercurial personality within your investor circle.

What you can expect from the process:

It will be extremely difficult to schedule an appointment with the hedge fund partner you have been introduced to. Often, they will only allow you to pitch your idea on the phone, and then, with blinding speed, they will say "Yes" or "No." With hedge fund partners, no means forget about it. If they say "Yes," then you can ask for an in-person meeting. This meeting will also be conducted at a blinding pace. Be prepared to compress your usual presentation into a fraction of the usual time it takes. If they are interested, they will expect to discuss the terms of investment at the first meeting and will often render a final judgment on the spot.

NARROWING DOWN YOUR BEST MATCH

Now that you have gained an understanding of the distinct classes of early-stage investors, let us dive a few fathoms deeper to study the different types of investors that exist within each separate class. If you are going to pinpoint your ideal investor, you ought to study them up close. Angel investors, because they are informally organized, tend to invest helter-skelter in a broad variety of business industries and therefore do not warrant a lot of close scrutiny. But for the more formal groups—like venture funds, strategic investors, and hedge funds—you can research the different firms to understand what types of businesses they partner with. You can begin to narrow your choices by finding the answers to a few basic questions.

First of all, does the firm prefer to invest in early, middle, or late-stage businesses? We have generally discussed the types of capital sources that are interested in early-stage businesses. However, even venture capital firms try to segment the market by choosing more precisely what early stage of development to invest in: seed stage, Series A, Series B, and so forth. Firms tend to stick to their preferences when it comes to preferred business-maturity levels. For example, if a venture-capital firm has invested heavily in very early-stage businesses, it specializes in early formation issues and has learned how to become successful in that niche. Therefore, the firm will most likely not be interested in more mature businesses, even if those businesses are still technically in the earlier stages of development.

Second, research what industries or types of business the investment firm has been successful with in the past. For example, if it is technology, is it software, hardware, social networking, or online gaming? Perhaps the firm specializes in real estate or retailing. Know what they like to invest in, and do not research this by asking the firm what they like. If you are a serious entrepreneur who has researched a unique idea and taken the preliminary steps to build a company, many venture capital firms will express an interest in meeting simply because they find your market attractive, regardless if they plan on investing in that industry now. They gain a valuable education, at your expense. If an investment group has never before invested in your market, it is not going to begin with your business, no matter what they tell you. A common trap that talented new entrepreneurs fall into is conducting a lot of unpaid training classes for uneducated investors.

The third question to ask in order to narrow your options is, what is the investment firm's business-driver expertise? If the potential investor you are researching has historically invested in retail chains that were driven by mass marketing and your retail chain is marketing-driven, then you have a direct match. However, if they invest in retail chains that find their success by undercutting everybody else's price, then you do not have a direct match. Perhaps they specialize in software technology that has national defense applications, or in understanding complex operating systems that can be made more efficient through automation.

They are, of course, far more likely to be interested in your business if it is not only the stage and industry they prefer, but they also have expertise in the basic drivers of its long-term success.

One additional piece of research that can benefit your targeting is to find out where the investment firm is in its own fundraising cycle. If its principals are out raising a new fund when you are about to meet them, they likely have almost finished investing out of their last fund. They may not be in a position to take on new investments (and, in any event, they are mostly focused on raising new capital, not investing in new companies). If, on the other hand, they have just completed raising a new fund, they will be anxious to get the money working in new investments. However, they will invest only in the exact type of investments they have promised their own investors they will make; there will be no exceptions in the early goings of a new fund. While this information can usually only be gained in a direct conversation with the investment fund, you can save yourself wasted time and effort by understanding whether the investment fund is itself in the early, middle, or late stage of development. Basically, if your business is an exact match for what they typically invest in, early stage is best. If you are quite close but not a perfect match, middle to late is better. If they are out fund-raising for their own new fund, do not bother until their fund-raising is complete.

CONCLUSION

It is a wonderful thing, really, that the world is full of investors and that they come in all sizes, shapes, and flavors. If you are a serious entrepreneur who has researched a unique idea and has prepared and organized to build a company around that idea, there already exists an investor that is your perfect match. If you can simply find that investor in time, he or she will be delighted to partner with you, and you will be launched. How will you find that one perfect investor? Naturally, you need to research the investor market, narrow the universe down to a small likely group, and then spend time getting to know the players within that group. In so doing, you will end up spending your time with investors who are genuinely interested in you and your idea. Better yet, they will be in a position to be helpful, whether they invest in your business or not. If you choose, however, to simply start knocking blindly on doors, expect to have a lot of doors slammed in your face, and perhaps to get bitten by the dog. Don't do that. Be nice to yourself. Take the time to find out where you are already wanted, then go there expecting and deserving a warm response.

ANGEL INVESTOR MYTH

"There are no angel investors in my area." Perhaps if you happen to live in the middle of the Australian outback, but otherwise, this is simply not true. Of course, you cannot open a phone book and look under *angel investors*. This type of investor is not recognized by any regulating agency, nor do they advertise in order to attract new businesses. A good starting point for ferreting out the angel investors in your area is to network with business colleagues, lawyers, accountants, college classmates, college professors, and even other start-ups. Simply ask who they might know with an interest in the type of business you are building, as you are looking for early-stage investors. If you keep asking, you will be amazed by the number of angel investors in your area.

Remember, angel investors are all around you. They are individuals who have an interest in particular types of businesses and have sufficient funds to be able to make the occasional opportunistic investment. They are people you rub elbows with in the business world every day. Do not get disillusioned by the non-transparency of the angel investors in your area; get busy networking. It is your job to find these people, it is not their job to be visible.

Dating Is Your New Job

As the founder and leader of your new business, you may have the noble vision of yourself as rallying the troops to charge into, do battle for, and ultimately conquer rich new territories that your business will then own. You are King Leonidas, leading three hundred Spartans into battle with the Persians in the movie *300*: fierce, heroic, iron-willed.

The role you need to prepare yourself for, however, is one that is much more familiar, if not nearly as heroic. The effective model for building your business is more like light-hearted romance than war. You are Bill Murray, in *Groundhog Day*.

After choosing the investor class, or classes, you think best fit your business, and targeting within those classes the specific investor firms or individuals that look like appropriate matches, you should have a collection of about ten high-probability investor options. Now, certain that you have good potential matches, you can afford to allot a significant amount of time to beginning a relationship with each investor. It would be unnatural if you were not somewhat nervous about how this process will develop. Fortunately, it is going to follow a pattern with which you already have experience. Developing a relationship with each investor is going to follow a path that is eerily similar to dating:

- You decide who you like (you did this in Secret 3).
- You get introduced.

- You date.
- You try to make it work.
- You break up (sad, but there is a valuable silver lining).
- You commit to a long-term relationship.

YOU GET INTRODUCED

In Secret 3, you learned how to edit your investor list down to the most probable matches. This is your list for introductions. Now you are to the point where you are interested in meeting them and seeing if the relationship has the potential to move forward. There are three important rules to remember during the introduction stage with investors:

> *Rule 1: No one is going to listen to you until you establish credibility.*
> *Rule 2: No one is ever going to call you back, ever.*
> *Rule 3: No one gets interested until they meet you in person.*

Almost none of your initial contacts with the investors on your list will be in person. In order to set up a face-to-face meeting, you will likely speak to the person on the phone, or, in some cases, your initial communication will be only via e-mail. Whatever the means of communication, the first thing to do when you actually talk to your targeted investor is to establish your credibility.

There are a few ways to build credibility when you first speak with a potential investor. First, you can simply introduce yourself—this will work if you happen to be Bill Gates, Warren Buffett, Barack Obama, or someone with similar name recognition and clout. If this is not the case, then you will need to borrow credibility from some person or firm that already has solid standing with your investor. For example, "Hi, Tom, it's Bill Fisher. I bumped into John

Cage, your CPA, and he encouraged me to give you a call about . . ."
This approach will be successful if you use anyone who has standing with the investor you are addressing. It may be a friend of the
investor, a former colleague, a nephew, a law firm, or simply a social contact that you have in common, such as a golfing or tennis
buddy.

Many countries are more hierarchical in their societal structure
than is the United States, which is presumed to be a fairly open soci-
ety. But wherever you find yourself, at this stage of the process it is
important to determine who is likely to be in your targeted investor's circle of influence before you talk to the investor. If you can find
a link through a business professor, then make an appointment
and go talk to that professor. If you know someone at the investor's
law firm, or in her social network, go and talk to that person.

Professional networking sites such as LinkedIn and Xing are
great tools for discovering common connections to business professionals. Even a simple Google search will often turn up common touchstones between you and your potential investor. By
researching targeted investors you will likely be able to see where
they have worked in the past and with which businesses they have
partnered. Chances are you will either know somebody at one of
these firms or know somebody who knows somebody at one of
these firms. A link is all you need. Most of the time, you will not
know you have the connection until you start doing your research.
Any common ground with your targeted investor can allow you to
borrow sufficient credibility. Finding and then referencing this
common ground at the outset of your initial conversation is essential to your prospects of starting a relationship.

If your initial communication is by e-mail, you will use the
same approach. Often your best tack, given how few e-mails are
read by their intended recipient, is to place the name of your legitimate reference point in the subject line, such as "Referral from Bill

Fisher." This will get your e-mail read, and it will be read precisely because you have borrowed sufficient credibility from that name to warrant the reader's attention.

Now we move on to rule number two: *No one is ever going to call you back, ever.* This is important because it is extremely difficult to time your initial call to the investor at the exact moment when he is available to talk. The universal tendency is to leave a message asking the investor to call you back. Or to accept someone's promise that the investor will call you back. He is not going to call you back, ever, and leaving a message asking him to do so leaves a weak first impression. The only information you should ever leave in a message for someone you have not met is:

1) The name of the person who is introducing you
   and
2) That you plan on calling him back at a different designated time.

If you are writing an e-mail, you probably already know that it is an easy medium to ignore, and you should not ask for or expect an answer to your e-mail. Simply mention the name of the person the investor knows who is introducing you, and tell her that you will call their office to set an appointment to talk.

Often, when you make the initial call to the potential investor, you will be connected with an assistant. Some assistants will relentlessly inquire about the nature of your call. In these cases, I strongly suggest that you use the name that helps to establish your credibility: "Please just tell Mr. Stevens that Pete Loran from Wells Fargo is connecting us, Pete Loran is the name he will know. Thank you." There is no other information that you can give that will be helpful at this point.

When you finally reach the investor, you will use the bullet-proof speech you learned how to develop in Secret 2 to introduce your reason for calling. But the initial call is only a prelude to scheduling a meeting with the investor. Remember rule number three: *No one gets interested until they meet you in person.* When you mention that you would like to schedule a meeting to explain your business, you will often hear from the investor, "Just send me your business plan, and we'll get back to you." This translates to "Make it easy for me to get rid of you." Do not be disagreeable, but do not ever believe that sending something will gain you an appointment. By now you know that—rule number two—this investor is not going to call you back, ever. Your best response is something along the lines of, "Of course, I'm happy to send you something, but I know you're not going to invest in a business plan, you would want to have confidence in the entrepreneur. I have some time this week, I could stop by for a coffee, what does your schedule look like?" No one is going to get seriously interested in investing in your business until and unless you meet in person. Be polite and be persistent. Offer to work around the person's schedule, offer to meet for a drink after work, offer to take him to lunch. Whatever it takes, make certain that you meet.

YOU DATE

Can you remember any of your first dates? Perhaps you have tried to forget. They are inherently awkward situations: two people meeting for the first time, both knowing they are going to take a few halting steps in a kind of ritual dance that may lead to a long-term relationship. First impressions matter in all arenas of dating, including business, and the impression you need to leave with your investor is that you know how to take charge of this potentially uncomfortable situation. Remember, you suspect you want this person as a partner; you are in pursuit. It is your responsibility to take the awkwardness out of the room, putting the investor at ease and moving confidently into your presentation. How will you do this? Well, just like in actual dating. You will start with light innocuous topics: the weather, the newspaper headlines, or the traffic on your way to the meeting. Once you are seated and ready to begin your presentation, you will put him at ease by asking him to first tell you a bit about his company and his background. An effective way to get them talking is to say, "I know we are here to talk about me and my business idea, but if you don't mind, since I don't know a whole lot about your firm, could you start by briefly telling me about Stradsworth Unlimited?"

Of course, he is made comfortable by telling you his story, which he has told hundreds of times before. As you listen, and interject occasionally with follow-up questions, you begin to get a sense of what kind of person the investor is. You get a feel for his language and the rhythm of his communication style. You can also hear in his descriptions of their business what things matter to him, the stature of his firm, the companies he has helped to build, the entrepreneurs he has helped to develop, and perhaps a few clues about his hobbies, or what kind of mood he is in.

Take note. All of this information will allow you, in your subsequent presentation, to be much more persuasive, as you stress the parts of your business that you now know matter most to him, as you reference his own language in order to explain some part of your business. Aim to move into a rhythm of presentation that is close to his chosen style. If you do not feel that you have gathered enough of this type of information from his initial response, you can always ask the additional question of how he got into the investing business himself. Again, this is a story he has told many times before, he likes telling this story, and you will gain valuable information if you are listening for the behavioral and intellectual clues that will help you understand how to become his partner.

As the investor talks, take written notes and let him see that you are taking notes. You will want to refer back to some of what he is telling you in your own presentation but also, just like in actual dating, the other person likes to know you are interested and listening.

If you have already taken the investor through your bulletproof speech, whether in an initial phone conversation or perhaps in a chance encounter somewhere, then the initial meeting in his offices will be the time to expand into your PowerPoint presentation. We have already discussed, in Secret 2, how to compose and present this incarnation of your story. You may want to bring along to this face-to-face meeting the three-year budget forecast as reference material that you can leave behind. But, if it has been properly composed, everything you need to discuss in this meeting is contained in, or closely related to, your set of PowerPoint slides. The meeting will most likely end with the investor saying some generally kind words about you and your business, and then telling you that he will give some thought to the material and call you back. But you know he will never call you back, ever. So you will end the meeting by reciting any follow-up information that you owe the investor in order to answer detailed questions he asked during the presentation. Then thank him for his time, and reaffirm for them why you think he could be an ideal investment partner for your business.

Lastly, you need to set the next appointment while you are with him. You can do this casually, as you are about to exit, by saying something along the lines of, "I know you've got some thinking to do, and we're both busy doing other things. Can we set a time now, say for a week from today, to get on the phone and talk about where you are in considering partnering with my business? What does your schedule look like next week?" Then set the appointment; do not leave this next step to chance. You are in front of the investor, in his office, he has just listened to your comprehensive, well-researched, and potentially lucrative business plan, and you have more than enough standing with the investor to ask for a follow-up appointment.

Before the next discussion date comes, you have work to do. To keep this person from forgetting about you altogether before the next scheduled talk, you need to remain a physical presence in his mind. In an actual dating scenario, you might send along flowers or a romantic follow-up note. I have never sent flowers to an investor, so I cannot say this would not work. However, what does work is to promptly send him any additional information you owe him in order to answer the questions raised during the initial presentation. If no additional information is required, you can pull from your catalog of pertinent articles discussed in Secret 2 as part of your essential kit. Send one of these articles to him with a note saying something like, "I know that we are going to be talking later in the week, but I came across this article and I thought it might interest you." This reminds the investor he has a follow-up date with you. Plus, it gives him more information that supports your business idea, but most importantly it reminds him of you. This is a nonintrusive, gracious way to stay in front of your potential investor.

When you do meet again, whether in person or on the phone, you will have passed into the second-date stage of awkwardness—more comfortable than the first date, but still awkward. Once again, it is your responsibility to take charge of the situation and put the investor at ease. You should begin by telling the investor that you enjoyed the initial discussion, with some real-life details as to why. Now you are interested in finding out the next steps in building a partnership. This gives the investor a platform on which to give you his considered feedback. At this stage, you will hear either a quick "No, we've decided we are not interested," or "We'd like to move ahead and understand more about your market, your budget projections, and so forth." The latter is the investor committing to the due-diligence phase of the relationship building. If the answer is "No," you should religiously follow the tips given in the section ahead in this secret entitled "You Break Up but . . ." If the answer is "Yes," he is going to move ahead, you are on your way. It may be that your next meeting is again in his office, but this time with several of his partners who want to meet you and hear your business story. Give the exact same PowerPoint presentation you gave to the initial investment partner. You do not need to worry that the initial partner, having heard your story before, will find this boring. He will remember very little or nothing about your presentation; he simply knows he was impressed with you and your idea and does not want to miss out on what may be a great investment. Everything else that you told him will most likely be forgotten. It has been my experience that, for a truly new business idea, the investors will need to hear the same story three or four times before it begins to sink into their memory.

Conclude this second PowerPoint presentation the same way you concluded the first one, and with the same emphasis on scheduling a follow-up date for further discussion.

If you are moving forward with the investor, there will be a series of meetings. Relationships take time. The only thing that can happen quickly is that the investor says "No." As long as you are not hearing no, the answer is yes, and you can continue to follow the general outline of this and the succeeding secrets until you close on your funding.

YOU TRY TO MAKE IT WORK

You and the investor are committing a lot of time and effort in this stage to trying to form a partnership. As you will note in the next secret, "Raising Capital Can Cost You Your Dream," you are also beginning to negotiate the early terms of your partnership, just as you would in an actual dating scenario. Beyond continuing to practice some of the dating dos and don'ts that have already been discussed, there are three important rules that now come into play:

> *Rule 1: No investor is ever going to do anything on time.*
>
> *Rule 2: You cannot have a long-term relationship until you learn how to disagree and still keep moving forward.*
>
> *Rule 3: Although you need money, you need money from a good, long-term partner, and for some inexplicable reason, God has chosen to order the world in such a way that there are a lot of jerks who have money.*

Rule 1: Investors are not going to accomplish any of their relationship-building tasks on time because, absent competition for potential ownership in your business, time is their friend. The longer they get to look at you, your business, the market, and so forth before committing, the more likely they are, in their way of thinking, to make a smart decision. Time, of course, is your enemy; you are already committed to this business, and you need a partner right now so you can start building. In order to manage efficiently through this part of the relationship building, you will need to create and manage your investor, as best you can, to a published timeline. Do so in such a way as to create the sensation of competition and a definitive deadline.

As soon as you can see that your investor is genuinely interested and is moving forward with due-diligence tasks, you should make this timeline a topic of conversation. In response to some positive remarks from your investor about you or the business, you will say something like, "That's great, we're looking forward to working through the process with you. Of course, you are a busy guy, and we are all busy, too, so I think the most efficient way to move forward will be if we can agree to a rough timeline of events." I would then hand your investor a timeline, penciled in with dates, that looks something like the following outline (except using actual dates rather than generic weeks).

Weeks 1–3: Meetings with high-profile investors
Weeks 4–6: Follow-up meetings
Weeks 7–9: Due-diligence activities and term-sheet discussions
Weeks 10–11: Term-sheet negotiations
Weeks 12–13: Transaction closing

Walk him through the steps. As you cover the items, you casually mention that you are meeting a number of potential partners just now, in this first phase, or perhaps that you are already in phase two and have multiple follow-up meetings going on with interested investors. Your potential investors will not see this as obsessive or cheeky behavior on your part. To the contrary, they will be impressed that you can organize a chaotic series of events into an orderly process and get things completed on time; it will only add to their confidence in you as a leader who can build a profitable business.

But the investor will not really want to follow the timeline, because, absent competition, time is their friend. Your timeline adroitly positions competition as part of the process, but you will need to constantly refer back to the timeline to keep the schedule moving forward. You can say things like, "I'm a bit worried that we're getting behind on our chosen schedule here. I know everyone is trying, but what can I or my team do to help keep the momentum going forward?" Referring to the published timeline, you can also say, "We're nearing the time now when we need to begin to talk terms with our chosen investor options, and I'd like to get a draft list of terms over to you or your attorney in order to stay on track." Putting the onus on the published schedule—and the need to stay on track—takes you out of the role of nagging and, instead, into the role of a busy executive, with a business to build, who is doing what's necessary to stay on a published schedule. Do not allow the schedule to become obsolete. If it needs to be reworked to allow for some inevitable delay—a disaster that understandably has delayed the process—announce that you will republish the schedule in order to reflect that reality but also in order to stay on track with the new deadline.

Of course, there can be no long-term relationship, no matter how efficient you are at moving through the timeline of relationship-building events, until and unless you learn how to disagree, and this is Rule 2 in trying to make it work. Disagreements are inevitable in business partnerships, just as in life partnerships and friendships. Think about the disagreements you have had with a significant other in your personal life. What worked? Perhaps you have more experience in what did not work, and that is essential information as well. The same set of behavioral guidelines you have painfully learned in the dating world will apply to building your investor relationships. As an example, issuing ultimatums, spending a lot of time pointing out why the other party is wrong, questioning motives, making frequent use of the word "No"— these work just as poorly in the business setting as you have found in the rest of your life. Instead, you are looking for common ground, trying to find the happy medium where you can agree. Demonstrate that you are willing to consider what is important to the other party, and try to be creative in finding ways to accommodate in these areas while, at the same time, not violating your own sense of fairness. Be diplomatic, albeit firm, when an important principle is at stake. And when one of your own important principles is being negotiated, it is healthy to ask the other party to be creative in finding a way to accommodate your issue. These early experiences with your investor will set the stage for how you can enter into a productive long-term relationship, and you should look at these early disagreements as creating a framework for joint decision making rather than some simplistic *I win/You lose* scenario.

Rule 3 is actually an encouragement for you to break off the relationship yourself if you come to find out, somewhere in the process, that your investor is a jerk. This may be the single hardest lesson for new entrepreneurs to grasp. You can expend so much time and energy getting ready to meet a suitable investor, and sometimes the need for that next round of capital is so overpowering, that it is a natural tendency to overlook really untenable faults before you tell the interested investor, "No, thanks." Or, worst of all, taking the money with the hope that the investor will become more manageable later. The best antidote to this tendency, to return again to the dating metaphor, is to understand that in this trying-to-make-it-work stage, the investor is on his very best behavior. If, on his very best behavior, the investor is already proving to be unruly, or untrustworthy, or insufferable in some other tangible way, it will only get worse later. Once you have taken his money, there is no turning back. Turn back now, even if it means you have to scale back your business plans in order to extend the available time for finding a suitable investor.

I have been fortunate to end up with mostly wonderful investors in my entrepreneurial activities, many of whom have become lifelong friends and longtime multifaceted business partners. But, of course, I have made this particular mistake of choosing a poor match as well—remember, I learned what I know by trial and error. It is almost impossible to describe the havoc that can be wreaked on a fast-growing business by having one rotten apple in the investor team. He holds everyone back. He can pick nonsensical fights with your other investors. When he does not get his way, he will lodge specious threats against the board, and he can ultimately derail your business—I have lived through all of this. Even if you manage your troublesome investor better than I did mine, it will take up an enormous and debilitating amount of time. If you already have enough experience with your potential investor to have worries that he will be a problem, he will be. While it may seem a small luxury, given the seeming scarcity of start-up investors for your business, remember that no one can invest in your private company without your express approval. You are in charge, and in a way that will seem unusually powerful should you ever manage, by contrast, a public company with free-market investors. Use your power: say no.

Even with the best of institutional investors, there is usually one member of the investor's team that you will meet during this due-diligence phase who will be difficult to manage. In the institutional investment firms, the most junior members, often the most recent hires, are assigned to accomplish some mechanical parts of the due diligence that the senior staff does not want to handle. These junior staff members rarely have any operating experience, are often newly graduated from an MBA program, and sometimes arrive from business school with a toxic mix of emotional themes. They have an inflated opinion about their business knowledge, and they are nervous about their jobs; the worst of these are generically referred to by serial entrepreneurs as "ankle biters." By questioning everything about you and your ideas, they sometimes think they impress their bosses with their own perceived wisdom. When this junior staff member is asking you about some obscure detail of your business in a condescending manner, resist the temptation to reach across the conference table and smack him. Instead, realize that he is an important part of the process, and, whatever your opinion of him happens to be, he is the one who is reporting back to the partner who will ultimately recommend the investment to his firm. My advice is to treat the junior staff member like a very bright pupil who is there to learn from you. Double-check their understanding about everything you tell him, and assign him additional areas of your business to research if you believe it can help in his overall business judgment. In those rare cases when you find that you simply cannot work with an obvious ankle-biter, go immediately to the investment partner and be frank about it. Ask for someone else to be assigned to your deal.

It is also worth noting that the senior member of the investment firm who spends a lot of time with you is your champion to the other members of his firm. When he is asking questions of you, or challenging your assumptions and projections, he is actually preparing himself to champion you and your business to his colleagues. Treat this senior person well. Give him all of the information he asks for, ask him where he sees weaknesses in your business model, and partner with him to strengthen the planning for those areas. It is your responsibility to arm your champion with sufficient confidence in your business prospects that he can be successful in persuading his firm to invest.

YOU BREAK UP, BUT . . .

Neil Sedaka's song "Breaking Up Is Hard to Do" was a hit because everyone could connect with its message. However, when your potential investor breaks up with you, although you will feel rejected, the breakup event presents a golden moment of opportunity for you to strengthen your business prospects.

If you have spent time in due diligence with an investor, the partner you have been dealing with will call you when the firm decides not to invest, and say some nice words about you and your business idea and then drop the hammer: "We've decided to not move forward with this investment. We appreciate your time, and we are returning all of the materials you have supplied us with." You will hear those words, your heart will fall, and like everyone else in the world, you will feel rejected. You have just been dumped. But, although you are in a state of mild shock, you are still on the telephone with the investor, so how should you respond?

Here our story departs from the usual romantic-dating scenario, because this moment of breaking up in a business setting presents a golden opportunity to meet your future ideal investor and to eliminate a glaring weakness in your business. But you will need to rise above your natural feelings of rejection, and this is difficult. Here is exactly what you say: "Well, of course I'm disappointed, but I wonder if in closing I could ask you a favor." The investor doesn't like making calls to desperate entrepreneurs telling them no, so of course the investor wants to lessen the obvious hurt of dumping you by doing you some small favor. You continue: "You see, you are a professional investor, and I'm not, and I'll bet you would know other early-stage investors who might be interested in our company, maybe competitors of yours or other firms you have coinvested with in the past. Who else can you think of that might have an appetite for partnering with my company?" Every time that I have lived through this breaking-up moment, and it has happened to me many times, the investor has always responded favorably to this request, and virtually all of the investors that I ended up closing a transaction with were introduced to me at this exact moment in the relationship cycle. The investor will give you priceless insights about particular firms that are very closely matched to your business idea. Most often, they will offer either to make the introduction or at least to allow you to use their name—building credibility for yourself, of course—when you call on the referred firm.

Now, do not stop being brave just yet, there is one more crucial bit of information to gain before you hang up and get out your handkerchief. Here is what you say at the end: "Thanks, I'll call them. Just one other thing. I know we're not moving ahead with your firm, but since you have spent a lot of time studying our business and the market, tell me: If there was one thing that we could change in our business model that might have caused you to stay interested, what would that one thing be?" You have on the phone an investment professional who has devoted a lot of time in studying you, your business, the market you are attacking, and your potential competitors. He may be the most knowledgeable resource you will ever find in learning how to strengthen your business. His advice, at this moment, will often turn out to be the precise missing link in your business that, when fixed, causes your next set of potential investors to write you a check. From my own personal experience, it is extremely difficult to behave in the way I have described when you have had an emotional letdown. But this opportunity will not return, so buck up. Gather this vital information as your just reward for all of the time and energy you have invested in the relationship. Then hang up and go have a stiff drink.

WHAT'S IT ALL ABOUT?

It may help you in planning your relationship building with investors if you can visualize a kind of dating engine, which is, for your business endeavor, a kind of capital-raising machine. Here it is in rough schematic form.

This diagram shows how entrepreneurs take their idea to the planning and research stage, tell their story to investors in a variety of investor appointments, and attempt to start building a

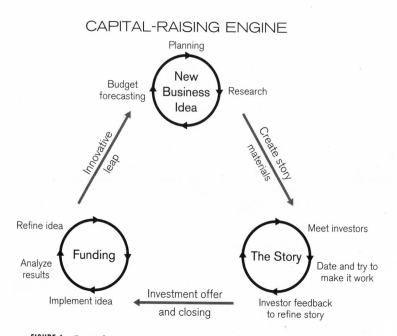

CAPITAL-RAISING ENGINE

Planning

New Business Idea

Budget forecasting

Research

Innovative leap

Create story materials

Refine idea

Funding

Meet investors

The Story

Analyze results

Date and try to make it work

Implement idea

Investment offer and closing

Investor feedback to refine story

FIGURE 1. Capital-raising engine taking ideas from planning to research.

relationship. When, inevitably, those early attempts do not work out, the entrepreneur creates a feedback loop, using both the new investor referrals and the feedback on critical fixes to the business model, then beginning again, repeating the cycle again and again, until the right business model meets up with the right investor and funding occurs. Funding of your early-stage business is not the goal, however; it is, as this schematic illustrates, only one more stop on a continuous loop of capital raising. The funds allow you to scale up your business, get into the market, and achieve some set of business results. For even the most mature companies, some part of this engine is always at work. Investor reaction is always shaping your ability to move your business forward into new territory, and business results are always informing and refining the shape of your basic business model.

CONCLUSION

Dating should be fun. It is inherently exhilarating to meet lots of new possible partners, learn about them, and teach them about your ideas. You have the opportunity to explore the possibilities that each partner may represent in helping you achieve your own goals, living through the many surprising twists and turns that attend any kind of relationship building. But it is only fun if you keep it in perspective. In the business setting, this dating phase is a learning cycle. It teaches you about the best investor matches for the next stage of your business evolution while at the same time informing you how to improve and alter your business model.

At some point in the process, your business model will be a perfect match for the investor you have been introduced to. But even then, that is not the finish line. It is one more stop on the circuit. Stay busy, stay focused, but do not strain. Learn to enjoy the community of useful business contacts you are building and the parade of colorful personalities that populate the investor universe. And keep in mind that this phase, while recurrent, is not continuous. Once you have found your ideal investor and funded the next stage of your business growth, then comes a level of partnership that precludes additional dating; you will be relatively monogamous. In retrospect you will find that you often look back at this dating phase and long for the freedom of possibility it offers.

INVESTOR DATING MYTH

When an investor drops you after serious consideration, your appropriate emotional response is to move on, thinking that they offer no additional value to your business building. Oddly, the exact opposite is true. The most valuable information you will receive in trying to raise capital will be available to you at the precise moment that the serious investor tells you that they are not going to invest. What is extremely difficult is to employ the discipline that enables you to ignore the obvious emotional letdown and, instead, bravely pursue referrals to other investors and tips on how to improve your business. But you have invested a lot of time and effort with this investor, and you have every right to expect some return on your investment. Most investors will be only too pleased to oblige, out of a feeling of respect for what you are trying to build.

Raising Capital Can Cost You Your Dream

After you have met hundreds of people and been bounced around from referral to referral to referral; after you have given scores and scores of presentations; after you have dated and then seriously dated several interested investors; after you have retooled your model and fixed all of the kinks that the different parties mentioned when you broke up—somebody is going to fall in love with you and your business idea. You are going to experience waves of joy when you hear from an interested investor who says she is going to make an offer.

You will be reaching for the champagne that you chilled months ago in anticipation of this moment. Your head will be in the clouds, and you will want to sit back with the bubbly and reflect on all the hard work you have put in. At many points along the way, you will have been plagued by self-doubts, about your business idea and about your own sanity in pursuing the idea of founding your business. Now someone is telling you that she believes in you and your business idea enough to write you a check for more money than you may have imagined was possible. You are already thinking about who to call first to spread the good news.

It is in this moment of elation that danger sets in. This transition, from dating to negotiation with your future partner, marks the turning point where, blinded by a sense of your own long-awaited success, you are most in danger of driving your dream off the road—or unwittingly handing the keys to the vehicle to your new investor. You may have heard horror stories of entrepreneurs who, despite building a great business, were thrown out by their investors, or denied their fair share of the economic rewards. When you enter the negotiation phase, you are on the platform where those horror stories first take shape, and you simply cannot afford to be in a merry, exultant mood. Getting funded ensures your business a future. But how you handle the negotiation of the investment terms will determine what say you will have in building that future, and how much of the economic value you will own. Recall that you are at a distinct disadvantage in this negotiation, because your investor has negotiated dozens of such transactions and you have negotiated probably a very small number, or none. You are the guy who walks into a high-stakes poker game and announces, by your own ignorance, that you want the seasoned poker players to teach you the game. They will.

You are allowed your moment of excitement. And then you need to get organized. Thankfully, in Secret 4 you have already learned how to create and introduce a timeline in order to take charge of the negotiation process. Bring this timeline forward as soon as your investor announces she wants to invest. Next, announce to your investor that you would like to get the important transaction issues set down on paper so you can both look at them and begin to agree on deal points.

THE NEGOTIATION DYNAMICS

Investors have their own best interests, and not yours, in mind. Their implicit goal in the negotiation is to give you everything you need—but not all that you want—in order to complete the deal, and keep the rest. You should have your own best interests in mind. Your goal is to give the investors everything they need—

not what they want—in order to complete the transaction and keep the rest for yourself. If this is a first-round funding, you likely own 100 percent of your business. Everything you give up in the coming negotiation—in voting rights, in management control, in economic ownership—will diminish your stake in the business you want to build. Of course, it is worth it, as you cannot grow your early-stage business without outside funding. But it is only worth it if you negotiate smartly on each issue, even if some of the issues are, in your first time around the fund-raising track, unfamiliar to you or seemingly esoteric.

An investor's needs can be broken down into two broad categories: economic needs and control needs. Think for a moment about what an investor would truly need in order to be fairly rewarded for the investment in an early-stage business like yours. They will include the following:

- A return on their investment, which should include some secured interest if the company fails. This fulfills their economic need.
- Some say-so in major decisions about how the company spends money. This fulfills their need for control.

One would think that, with such a short and basic agenda, the deal points to be negotiated would be blessedly brief. But brief they are not. Over the history of venture investing, deal terms have become ever more specialized, branching out from these two essential needs like manifold tributaries from a great river.

Now that we have surveyed the basic needs of your investor, and established the volatile negotiation dynamics, let's begin to learn how to negotiate the important issues in a healthy, wholesome, and dispassionate manner. How you negotiate does not matter just because of your ability to achieve the desired business outcome.

How you negotiate also matters because, when this transaction closes, you will have a new partner to work with, and you cannot afford to poison that relationship in the course of negotiating your deal.

In the following sections, I have placed the primary negotiation arenas in rough descending order of importance. Not every item that you will be asked to negotiate is listed, but rather the critical ones that are customary. As we have already discussed, you will need to engage a law firm to help in this negotiation, and that firm will be worth its weight in gold if you manage it correctly. But you must understand the major issues well enough to direct your attorney in what you are trying to accomplish. Do not delegate this negotiation. At any major point of the process, if you find the attorney is directing the agenda, remind yourself that you are now at risk of losing long-term value in your company—not because your attorney is incompetent, but because this is not the attorney's company, the attorney does not even own shares in your company, the attorney is being paid by the hour. It is your company, and this negotiation, this particular moment in time, is when a big part of your future and your company's future will be decided.

ECONOMIC NEEDS

Valuation (Price per Share)

Once you ask for a specific dollar amount from an investor, the first question that will be going through her mind is, "At what valuation?" The answer dictates the percentage of your business that your investor will own in return for her cash. For example, if you ask for $150,000 and your initial valuation for your business is $300,000, then you are offering your investor one-third of your business. (The cash that is invested is always added to your initial valuation. The calculation is done as follows: $300,000 plus $150,000 = $450,000 divided by $150,000, which equals one-third.)

Because the initial valuation you establish in your first round of funding has such far-reaching consequences to your business-building, we are going to slow down here and examine each aspect of this topic. No point of your business agreement will be more fiercely negotiated, and no other point will have such a profound and pervasive impact.

The initial valuation is what you can demonstrate your fledgling business is worth today. In the case of a mature business, the valuation would be established by some multiple of your realized earnings: a high multiple for a high-growth business, a low multiple for a steady slow-growth business. As an early-stage business, you do not have earnings. You likely do not even have revenues. As a result, your initial business valuation is an educated estimate.

Many start-up valuations will be calculated by deriving the net present value of your future projected cash flows. The net present value calculation uses a discount rate based on the time value of money (because of inflation, it becomes less valuable over time). The future cash flows of the business, and the value (multiple) of those cash flows that the wider market will place on your business, will always dominate the valuation negotiation. As we discussed in Secret 2 in the section entitled "Your Three-Year Budget Projection," the investor will rigorously investigate every fact and assumption that informs your business projections, and they are motivated, in some ways, to be more pessimistic about the business prospects than you are.

For start-ups, not having a business history is a mixed blessing. Absent a genuine business track record, all of your projections are open to debate. However, absent a genuine business track record, there are few direct facts to refute your projections. This, once again, places a premium on the strength of the research that underpins the primary drivers of your business model success. But in a small yet decisive way, it also allows your personal belief in what will happen to play a role in the negotiation. When your business has matured, and a pattern of hard factual results rules your forward projections, the importance of your business vision will diminish if not disappear altogether. Most entrepreneurs start their businesses out of a conviction that there is some inefficiency or inequity in the current market that can be made better. This conviction will have its greatest power to persuade investors—to be, in effect, irrefutable—in the early stages of business financing. Use it wisely.

Your initial business valuation is important not simply because it defines how much of your business (one-half, one-third, 80 percent) you will trade away in return for the investor's first round of cash. It is likewise important because your initial valuation will exert a long-term gravitational pull on all the future valuations of your business, those that will be negotiated in future rounds of financing. Each of these succeeding financings will shave off an additional piece of the business you own and hand it to the new investor in return for her cash; the size of that piece will be a direct outcome of the agreed valuation. Here is how you are forever tethered to your first-round valuation. Let us say that you agree to an initial valuation of $1 million, and your first-round investor invests an additional $1 million in cash; she owns 50 percent of your business on day one.

After you have implemented your business plan by hiring employees, producing a product, gaining some early customers, and so forth, you will then go back to the market to raise a second round of capital in order to continue to grow your promising but still unprofitable business. The next investor will proceed through all of the steps outlined in this book in coming to a determination of whether or not to invest. If the decision is in favor of it, this new investor will always look at the last-round valuation as an important and usually dominant factor in deciding the new-round valuation. The thinking goes something like this: the initial round valuation was $2 million, the business has accomplished all these important milestones in the subsequent time frame, and so the investor believes you have doubled, or perhaps tripled, the value of the company from where it started.

The math will always be anchored to the first-round valuation as the primary driver of the new-round valuation. I have experienced this in building my own business. In my first company, I had an early offer from one of the world's most prestigious institutional investors to invest $1 million at a post-money valuation of $2 million. Because the glorified name of this investor would have added great value to my business, I seriously considered taking that offer. But I ended up deciding to pass on what I believed was a too pessimistic view of my business. Ultimately, I secured an opening investment of $2 million from two large blue-chip institutional investors at an initial valuation of $6 million, which means that they owned 25 percent of the business (6 plus the 2 in cash = 8 divided by 2 = 25 percent). Of course, anyone can understand the basics of why the second offer (25 percent versus 50 percent) was a better one for my economic return as an entrepreneur. However, it is what happened next that illustrates what we have been discussing.

In the second round of financing for that same company, the investors looked at all the company had accomplished—hiring employees, building a first-of-its-kind online product, testing the customer demand in major marketing pilots—and decided that they would double the initial valuation of the company. The company's value grew from $8 million to a pre-money valuation of $16 million, and my investors then put in what was $3 million to own 3/19ths of the company. For two rounds of financing, totaling $5 million, I had traded away approximately 41 percent of the business. If I had taken the initial offer at a $2 million valuation, not only would I have given up 50 percent of my business on day one, but in the succeeding round, I would have traded away an additional 3/7ths of my business for the additional $3 million. Total raised in this example would have been $4 million, for which I would have traded away 92 percent of my business. This is a devastating result on the face of it, but the raw math grossly understates the loss, since 92 percent of the voting control would now be in hands other than mine, meaning that I would no longer control my own business. I now exist in the business's decision making only at the whim of my investors: game over, dream lost.

Your budget projections, as outlined in Secret 2, will have already nominated your opening assertion on the initial valuation of the business. When the actual negotiation begins, the investor will begin to question your calculations. Do not tremble; you have done your research, and you know not only how this can play out but also why it is all important for you to work through the process. First, you must pinpoint exactly why the investor believes that the ultimate valuation of your company will be lower than you believe it will be. Do the two of you differ on the size of the market, on your ability to capture profitable market share, or perhaps on how long it will take to build a viable company? Whatever the reason, you should now be just as diligent in questioning the investor's sources of information and research as they have been about yours. Recall that yours is an early-stage business, with few if any operating results to refute your assertions. The difference between you and your investor must owe to conflicting research. Do not assume that the investor, because of her swagger, knows something that you do not. Just keep questioning what leads her to believe differently than you. If you find that their research has uncovered some decisive bit of information that you were unaware of, naturally you need to agree and make an appropriate adjustment to your valuation and move on. But if you find instead that you simply have different sources of information on the same topics, you can negotiate as an equal.

For most situations, the only other negotiating maneuver you have in this sensitive valuation dance is to adroitly suggest the presence of other potential investors, investors that may have a more confident view of your business. You cannot confront your negotiating investor with this potential competition unless there are, in fact, other potential investors you are talking to (which is one reason, among others, to always be talking to more than one potential investor). You should never mention the name of the other investors, as investors are always capable of calling each other and talking shop without you in the loop. Nor should you make any threats. You simply want your investor to understand that, while you do want to get a deal done with her, it needs to be fair, because you have other options.

Preferred Shares

Until you are a public company, virtually all of your investors will invest only if they receive preferred shares. This means that, in addition to the price per share, which is the same as the price for the common shares, the preferred shares have certain rights that place them ahead of other shares (some of which will be explained in the sections below). The fact that your investor requires preferred shares is not negotiable. The type and degree of their preferences is where most of the negotiation action takes place.

Liquidation Rights

Under the umbrella of an investor's economic needs are liquidation rights. Your investor believes that, if the business fails for some unforeseeable reason and is sold below some targeted rate of return for the investor, she should then receive a multiple of the cash she invested. This return will be at the expense of the other investors (and you) in return for her having given you the chance to succeed. She will suggest a multiple—two times her original investment back, or three times in the case of business failure. Your position as the entrepreneur is that everyone is sharing risk by investing in the business. In your own case, in addition to whatever cash you have contributed, you have invested your own reputation as well as your time and sweat. As a result, you reason with the investor, although you appreciate her investment dollars, she should not be expecting special treatment in the event of failure, much less if it comes at the expense of others who took similar or even greater risks.

To find the proper point of compromise, take the position that the investor will be allowed to get her original cash investment back before anyone else gets a return of their invested capital. That gives the investor a small but meaningful preferred return.

Dilution Protection

If the company should ever need to sell subsequent shares at a price lower than today's price, your investor will typically ask to be protected from dilution. Dilution occurs when an investor ends up owning an ever smaller percentage of your company as you take on new investors down the road. Her position will be that, if you do a poor job in building the company, the amount and cost of capital required to complete the building process will go up. Therefore, when and if additional investors are brought in, you may need to induce them to invest by offering a price lower than today's price. Your early investor will want you, other founders, the management team, and perhaps other investors lesser than they are, to take most or all of the resulting dilution. Specialized language has emerged to describe distinct methods of distributing the dilution risk among investors. At the moment I am writing this, the common terms are *full-ratchet*, *weighted average*, and *broad-based weighted average*. Your position as the entrepreneur will be that the investor is putting capital into a high-growth business that has the potential for a high return. With that potential high return come risks of many kinds, including the risk of dilution. Further, you will argue, you want her as a member of the team, not as an isolated figure in the business. If the team, as guided by the board, decides that the business will need more investment capital, and that the price of capital, due to unforeseen circumstances, should be set lower than today's price, then everyone on the team should take the dilution equally.

Dividend Rights

Professional investors will often ask to receive a dividend on their investment. The dividend will take the form, as it does for public stocks, of a percentage of the purchase price of the stock, say 3 or 4 percent per year. As the entrepreneur, you will find this negotiating point hilarious, as your company, at this fledgling stage, is the farthest thing imaginable from a large, successful public company able to pay dividends out of excess profit. You can compromise by offering to accrue—not to pay but to recognize as an obligation to pay—the dividend, year after year. However, you should not agree to pay the accrued dividend until there is a public offering or a sale of the company, at which time you will find it relatively painless to settle accounts.

Investment Rights

If additional funds are going to be raised in order to fund your company's growth, your early investors may argue that they should have the right, but not the obligation, to put in these additional funds. In this way they reserve the right to own an ever-greater percentage of what is, by definition—if they choose to invest—a growing success. Their position is that this is part of their reward for taking the risk of being the early investor.

Your position should be that you will need freedom to attract a variety of investors into the business to be certain of finding the funds you need. After all, these original or early investors' funds are not limitless. Also, as importantly, you will want this freedom in order to attract the variety of business skills and advice necessary for balanced business decision making as you continue building the business. You can compromise on this point by offering your early investors the right to invest sufficient funds, in subsequent rounds of capital raising, to maintain their percentage ownership of the business.

Co-sale Rights

Co-sale rights explain what happens if you should ever decide to sell some of your shares to an outside party before the investor has had the opportunity to receive a cash return on her investment. The investor would like to be able to sell the same number of shares as you are selling and at the same price.

Attorney Fees and Transactions

Other economic needs that investors will find important are attorney fees and transaction fees. One of the most difficult ideas for me to fathom in my first time around the capital-raising track was that the investor's attorneys would work tirelessly throughout the negotiation to outfox my attorneys and me. And then, when the transaction was nearing a successful closing, the investor's attorneys would be paid out of the proceeds of the investor's initial investment, which meant *I* would pay *her* attorneys! I suggest not thinking about this too much, as you will go blind.

The best way to understand this is, it is the custom. However, that does not mean that the amount paid to the investor's attorneys is not subject to negotiation. The investor will argue that you must cover 100 percent of her attorneys' fees. As the entrepreneur, you will argue that since you have no control over her attorneys, you cannot be held responsible if her attorneys overcharge, overcomplicate, or otherwise muck up the whole transaction. You can propose a cap of some reasonable number (your own attorney will have a number in mind), and beyond that cap the investor is responsible.

Transaction fees are equally hard to fathom. But it has also become the custom for some investors to try to book an immediate return on their invested funds by charging a 1–2 percent transaction fee, which they argue is the cost of their manpower invested in due diligence and negotiation. This fee, again, comes out of the proceeds of their investment in your company, before you see their money. In effect, you are being asked to pay them for the time it took them to decide to invest in your company.

If the investor is intractable on the issue, you can propose that, at the very least, the amount of the total investment should be grossed up so that the company receives the nominated amount after the fee is subtracted.

SUMMARY OF ECONOMIC ISSUES

Although the language and nuance of these economic issues may be abstruse, you can see clear negotiating themes emerging in the scenarios outlined above. In general, the investor has the incentive to focus on risk, and in general you as the entrepreneur have the incentive to focus on opportunity. In general the investor is also inclined to argue that she deserves special treatment. But, in general, you as the entrepreneur are moved to maintain that she is joining a team, and the treatment of team members should be balanced and fair. You will never be as expert in understanding the finer points of these economic issues as your investor. But you have a negotiating position that she will never have: you are the leader of the business, building a team, and teamwork requires fair play. How you use this negotiating position will determine your own economic future in the business you are building.

CONTROL ISSUES

The second broad category of investor needs is control—broadly speaking, control of how their cash is going to be used to grow the value of the business. Of course, it is natural that the investor should have some protection in the event of outright fraud, or even from her cash simply being frittered away. How much protection, and what form that protection should take, is where all of the negotiation action will take place on these issues. What follows below is a list of the most common control issues to be negotiated with investors, along with a brief explanation of the issue, why it matters, and how to find a compromise.

Voting Rights

Each class of shares (series A, series B, common, and so forth) may end up with different voting privileges as part of that class of stocks' "preferences." Your investors in an early-stage business would prefer that their chosen class of stock have voting privileges that are superior to all other classes. For instance, each share counts for two votes, or ten votes, versus your common shares, which only get, say, one-for-one treatment. Your position as the entrepreneur is that you do not want one class of shareholder to run the company; the board should be running the company along with the management team. As part of the board (if you have granted her a board seat), your investor will already have sufficient voice in influencing the company's decisions. In cases of extreme entrepreneur leverage, that is, when many more investors want to own the stock than you as the entrepreneur need, the entrepreneur may negotiate that founder shares outvote all other classes of shares. By law, however, many corporate issues must be put to a shareholder vote, and so this issue of voting rights is not inconsequential. You can compromise by giving your investor some veto rights on decisions that can be harmful to her own economic position. With that said, I would strongly advise not to ever give broad-based voting preferences to your investors. If you do, you will find that, at decisive moments in the business evolution, they are running the company, not you.

Protective Provisions

Protective provisions prevent the new investor from losing the preferences they have negotiated with you during this round of investment by a subsequent vote of all the shareholders you may someday have in the business. Within reason, you as the entrepreneur should be agreeable to these protective provisions.

Major Expenditures

It makes sense for your investors to have input about major expenditures that the company will make. What will not work is for them to have so much control that your hands are tied in running the day-to-day business. Investors will sometimes ask for veto power over any expenditure exceeding some very low number, say $50,000. They still believe that it is their cash and they should be able to dictate how it is spent. Your position, as the entrepreneur, is that they are investing their cash in return for stock in the company. Therefore, they have all the rights a shareholder is entitled to. As regards expenditures per se, the company has an annual budget, which is approved by the board. The proper point of compromise when negotiating major expenditures is that you can offer to give the investor some veto power over major expenditures that are not in the approved annual budget.

Budget Approval

For the same reasons as outlined above, the investor may try to obtain veto power when it comes to overall budget approval. Your position as the entrepreneur is that the board has responsibility for overseeing budget approval. If the investor is not going to be granted a seat on the board, it is probably reasonable to give him some consultation rights on budget approval, but only as part of the normal board-approval process.

Approval Rights on Sale of Company/IPO

Investors will often ask for veto power on the sale of the company or the timing of an IPO. Your position as an entrepreneur is that the board is legally responsible for approving the sale or IPO, and, if the investor is a part of the board, he already has input. A point of compromise can be to give the investor some veto rights if the company is going to be sold or taken public below a stated price. This price, which will also be a source of negotiation, should be computed in such a way that the investor has veto rights only if the sale of the company is going to result in his achieving a substandard return. On anything above that price, the board will have final authority.

Information Rights

Professional investors will require that you regularly publish for them the financials of the company, standard profit and loss, and balance sheet accounting. Of course, the investor will want to know that you will be a good steward of her investment dollars. He will want to see that the progress of the business, in achieving targets on revenue, expense, and even profit, is being accurately reported and on a timely basis. This is reasonable.

For a start-up company, it is typically unreasonable for the investor to require audited financials except perhaps on an annual basis. The investor would prefer that you agree to provide financials audited by a top-five accounting firm, PricewaterhouseCoopers or KPMG, for instance. But you will find that those firms are very expensive for a start-up, and there are plenty of solid, smaller, regional accounting firms that can work at rates you can afford. An important note about choosing your accounting partner: You as the entrepreneur may prefer that your financial statements be prepared by your brother-in-law or, better yet, your mom, as they will have your best interests at heart in the way the numbers are reported. Do not take this approach. Get a professional, no-nonsense accounting firm to compile your quarterly and annual financial statements. As an entrepreneur, you are going to have moments in the topsy-turvy world of building a business when the pressure on you to produce favorable numbers will be so incredibly intense that you will be tempted to somehow fudge the score in order to meet expectations. Every business leader feels this temptation in certain high-pressure moments. Furthermore, financial reporting, for a private company, is a complex field with many byzantine rules, which can lead to unintended opportunities to "manage" the numbers. Fudging the numbers, even ever so slightly, will *always* turn out to be a mistake. You need to put yourself on a short leash when it comes to reporting the numbers. A professional outside accounting firm will save you a lot of unnecessary headaches because that firm is not going to put up with any of your creative accounting ideas.

Founders Vesting

As the entrepreneur, you have believed that one of the rewards for doing all the incredibly hard work of breathing first life into the lungs of your business was that you would own most of the stock, at least at the outset. The investor, however, views this as a risk. He believes that if you already own most of the stock, you could easily find it to your advantage to leave the business early and collect your winnings out of the hard work that the remaining team, including your investor, produces. The investor is, in part, investing in your ability to build the business and wants you tied firmly to it all the way up to the point when she, the investor, gets a return on her investment.

A principal point of negotiation will be how much of the stock that you thought you already owned is going to be subject to vesting (usually a time schedule for ownership) and on what terms. As you see, you do not own all of your stock in return for having brought the business to life. Instead you own certain rights that may allow you to own that stock if you stick around to build the company. You will never win the argument that none of your stock should be subject to vesting, so focus on how the stock will vest, and perhaps how much will be subject to vesting. The investor would prefer, of course, that all of your stock be subject to vesting and that your stock only vests after some long time frame, say five years. You, on the other hand, prefer that most of your stock vests almost immediately. The right compromise is to agree to receive some portion of your stock with immediate vesting in return for your founding efforts. The remaining stock vests as you spend time in building the business, say every month, over a likely amount of time for the business to achieve some financial success, say thirty-six or forty-eight months. You will maintain, however, that all of your stock should vest immediately if the company is sold or goes public (because this means you must have done a good job in building in the company, no matter when it occurs). You will also maintain that all of your stock should vest immediately if you are terminated without cause (see employment section for the ironies of agreeing to be terminated without cause by the business you founded).

Approval Right on Liquidation

Investors will often ask for veto power over a liquidation of the business, which can result in bankruptcy, sale on behalf of creditors, and so forth. Once again, your best argument is that this is a matter that the board is responsible for deciding. A point of compromise would be to offer the investor a provision that the company cannot be liquidated unless a reputable accounting firm judges the firm to be "not a going concern," a formal accounting judgment that a business is going to fail.

Compensation of Senior Managers

From the investor's point of view, it would be best if all members of senior management were willing to work without salary but rather simply for the appreciation in stock price that will result from those senior managers' efforts. This is in the best interest of investors because it is the only way they make money. As a practical matter, this arrangement does not attract quality managers. But investors will often ask for veto/approval power over the compensation of the firm's senior managers—say the top three to five most highly compensated executives. This essentially gives them the power to prevent cash from being taken out of the company by overpaying its managers. Your position, as the entrepreneur, should be that you must be allowed to pay market rates for top talent; otherwise the business cannot grow. A point of compromise can be to offer the investor some approval rights over your own compensation, and/or to include board approval of, say, the top three most highly compensated executives in the company.

Use of Proceeds

You are essentially promising to use the money the investor is contributing to grow the business rather than, say, to take your girlfriend on a week-long sailboat cruise down the Dalmatian coast. If you decide to go on the sailboat cruise anyway, buy the boat, do not rent it, because you will not be coming back.

Board Representation

The board of directors of your company will allow you a forum to receive impartial advice from seasoned business leaders, and the board will also have a legal responsibility for the company's major decisions. However, because so many strategic decisions are reserved to the board's judgment, smart investors often try to make the case that they deserve outsized representation on the board. In so doing, they try to gain control of the company's decision making. The case usually made by such investors is that, because they are the first institutional investor to come into the business (or because of the size of their investment or the prestige of their firm), they should be granted, say, three board seats out of a total of five members.

You should never agree to this proposition, for reasons that are not entirely obvious. Of course, at three of five they can outvote everyone on each important issue, and so they would be running the business. But even if they occupy only two of the five votes, this representation turns out to be actual flesh-and-blood board directors on your board, not simply numbers on a voting grid. Those two board directors will be much better at swaying the other members of the board to their, perhaps, self-serving positions if there are two of them lobbying as opposed to only one. And while you are focused on all the operational details of running the business, these directors may have few demands on their time other than furthering their own agenda in the business.

Furthermore, decisions made by the board, after documented deliberation, are almost unimpeachable by the legal process. Giving your investor outsized board presence can quickly turn your business, in all its most important aspects, into a kind of wholly owned subsidiary of the new investor.

A point of compromise, for a very large prestigious investor, might be to offer her one board seat, and then to say that the two of you—you as the entrepreneur and she as the investor—will jointly name a third independent director.

Board Makeup

Owing to its importance in the overall business-building process, the makeup and management of your board deserve their own separate secret. However, a few simple rules can help you to achieve an efficient board structure and operation in the early going. First of all, you as the entrepreneur must always be on the board; otherwise you would not even be present when the major decisions are taken. At the outset, you should always choose to be the chairman of the board as well. The chairman of the board has additional control rights that will be important in shaping the decisions on how you grow your business. As regards the size of the board, my own rule for start-ups is the smaller the board the better. You, the initial investor, and one outside director is perfect. However, if you are going to have two investor directors, I would strongly recommend you move to five directors: you, two outside directors, and the two investor directors to avoid overbalancing the board with investor issues.

When you agree to give a board seat to your investor, you should retain approval rights over which person they select to put on the board. You are going to spend a lot of time with that person, and personalities matter, particularly in small companies. You want someone you can get along with, but also someone who is going to bring an extra dimension of value to building the business. Ideally you want someone with a Rolodex of important business partners or years of experience building businesses similar to what you are now building.

Amount of Money You Invest

The more sophisticated the investor, the more they will want to focus on how much you, as the entrepreneur, have invested in the business. The investor is legitimately concerned about your commitment to the business, and knowing that you have invested your own money partially answers the question. Because most first-time entrepreneurs are not among the world's richest people, you may not be in a position to express your commitment by writing a check for $1 million to your company. Your position should be that, in addition to whatever hard cash you may have invested, you have also foregone wages during the business formation period. For this figure you should determine what your normal earnings might have been for that period and include any likely bonus you would have been earning. This can be a sizable number.

Your Employment Contract

If you are going to work inside the company you are building, you will want to have a well-thought-out employment agreement. A detailed employment contract offers comprehensive protection of your own business interests, and it will prompt your investors to take an interest in negotiating key terms.

The employment contract should detail the duration of your employment. Investors are likely to opt for a short term—one year or so—with renewable clauses, as this gives them greater flexibility over the leadership of the business. Your position should be that—as the founder, leader, and most significant shareholder— you need to know you have at least long enough to build the business into a viable long-term concern. Five years is best, but as a rule you should not settle for anything less than three years.

The contract will detail your salary. As previously mentioned, in the section above on compensation of senior managers, investors would actually prefer that you work without a salary. This would ensure that your only compensation would be perfectly aligned with theirs: turning the business into a profitable engine. In the actual event, the investor will admit you should be paid something, but at a level that will have you eating beans, not steak. Your position should be that you are not asking for anything other than market rate for your services.

Your employee contract should detail termination guidelines, because you cannot afford for your ability to build the business to rest on the whim of investors. Of course, there are instances that you can agree would trigger cause for termination, but when the game is played out, you will find that the definition of "cause" is all important. Investors will typically argue for a broad definition of cause (e.g., negligence, failure to achieve necessary business goals, not standing at attention when they pass by), as it gives the investor more flexibility in getting rid of you if they do not like the way the business is growing. Your position on the definition will be the polar opposite: an extremely narrow and high bar for cause (e.g., gross negligence, repeated failure to follow the written directives of the board, conviction of a felony). The consequences of this negotiation are serious. In most cases, if you are terminated for cause, the company does not owe you any severance, any accrued bonuses, or any unvested stock, and you might even have to divest yourself of stock you already own. In addition to your operating position, you might have to give up your seat on the board, and termination for cause will not enhance your business resume.

Your termination guidelines should detail the provision of termination without cause, which is not as far-fetched a scenario as it sounds. Many first-time entrepreneurs would maintain they could never be terminated from their own companies *without cause*. This is precisely why you want to spell this out in your contract. One day, someone may own enough shares in your company, or have control of enough votes on the board, to kick you out simply because they do not like you. Over time you are going to have a lot of investors in your business, and it is a certainty that someone, somewhere, is going to decide they just don't like you. When this happens you need to know how you are protected. Your protection is to make termination without cause extremely expensive for the investors and the company. Your employment contract should specify that termination without cause will require the company to pay you several years' severance, including an expected bonus, immediately vest to you any unvested shares, lift any noncompete and nonsolicit strictures, and allow you to retain your seat on the board.

Faced with these costs, the board will be hard-pressed to ever vote to terminate you without cause, no matter how great the pressure from some influential investor. But if for some reason they do, you are probably going to come out fine.

Your employee contract should detail the effect on your business interests triggered by your voluntary and involuntary resignation. Typically, the penalty involved in your voluntary resignation will mirror whatever you agree to in the event that you are terminated for cause. Just as you wanted the investors to feel the pain if they ever terminated you, your investors rightly want you to feel a lot of pain if you decide to walk away.

You can negotiate terms for involuntary resignation, which is a fancy way of saying the company somehow, in some way made the work environment too hostile for any reasonable person like yourself to want to stay. This could be a result of a salary cut, a demotion to a lesser position within the company, a loss of budget authority, and so forth. Terms for your involuntary resignation should closely mirror the terms that you negotiate for termination without cause.

Your employment contract should detail any noncompete and nonsolicit prohibitions. The investors want to know that you will not be able to take their money, start building the company, and then leave to go build a competitor using the ideas that you learned at their expense (this is the noncompete). Of course, they do not want you to do this by taking along the employees you hired and trained at their expense (this is the nonsolicit). These are reasonable concerns.

Taken together, the employment contract ingredients outlined above have the potential to cast a long and paralyzing shadow on all other control issues in your business operation. Get an employment contract negotiated with your investor, and get the protections you need in order to build the business without looking over your shoulder.

Negotiation Dos and Don'ts

If you have not had experience in business negotiations, you should expect to be overwhelmed, which will make it likely that you will overlook business terms that are extremely important to you and your future. Furthermore, as previously mentioned, you are at a distinct disadvantage: your investor has negotiated many early-stage company investments, and you have not. The following list of tips, rigorously followed, can act as a protective armor to see you safely through this stage of raising start-up capital.

- Get all of the issues on the table first; do not negotiate piecemeal. All of the business terms are relative, one to another, and putting them all within view allows you, and your investor, to see the big picture and to set an agenda for how to work through, item by item, to an eventual agreement.
- Draft and issue the initial term sheet. Investors will sometimes maintain that they should draft the term sheet, but they are often negotiating multiple deals simultaneously, so letting them lead will delay the process. By drafting one with your attorneys first, you set the framework for what will be negotiated.
- Give yourself time to consider what the investor is proposing, rather than agreeing or disagreeing on the spot. Remember you are a novice at negotiation; you need time to think things through. You will simply say, "OK, let me think about that and come back to you with my thoughts."
- In the course of the negotiation, for anything significant that you agree, at the investor's request, to give up, you will always ask for something in return. The way this will play out is that, after you have thought about their request, you will say something like, "I think I could get comfortable agreeing to your request on X if you would consider agreeing to allow me Y on business term Z." Be fair-minded in asking for a movement on their part similar to what you are offering to do in agreeing to their request: if they ask for a penny, do not ask in return for a thousand dollars, and don't do the opposite either.

- You address in your negotiation the things they need, not the things they want. An example can be seen in how to approach some business term that your investor is asking for and that you find objectionable. Rather than saying you cannot agree to what they are proposing, you want to say, "Tell me, what is it you are trying to accomplish with this term?" Often, their goal will turn out to be a complete surprise to you, and not at all obvious from their initial request. When you establish their goal, try to give some thought as to how you can allow them to accomplish it in a different way without your agreeing to their initially objectionable request.

- Always be diplomatic in your disagreement: Do not say, "No"; say, "I'm not sure if I could get comfortable with that." Do not say, "You're out of your mind"; say, "I'm not quite sure how you would have come to that conclusion." Do not say, "If I hear one more ridiculous comment come out of your venomous mouth, I'm going to get up and walk out and never come back;" say, "You know, it has been a long day, and we're making a lot of progress here. Let's take a thirty-minute break, shall we?" Just as in your personal relationships, how you learn to disagree with your investor and still keep moving forward will define, in large part, your future business relationship. Polite, firm, decisive, that is you.

- Whenever possible, try to disagree by disagreeing with your investor's advisers, such as their attorneys. By doing so you shift the disagreement away from being personal. You may say something like, "I know your attorneys are working very hard to protect your interests, but I think they have gone too far on this particular issue." For some unknown reason, all investors find it reasonable that you would blame their attorney for bad behavior.

- If it is a multiparty investment, pick a lead investor and negotiate only with that person and then announce the negotiated deal with all the other parties. Go so far as to give the lead investor additional benefits in the deal in order to motivate them to take this leadership position. Never, ever negotiate with multiple parties simultaneously. I believe that psychiatric wards are filled with examples of what this activity will do to your mind.

- People are human, and the best of them have the potential, at some point, to become fatigued and then give up on negotiating. You cannot afford to let this happen. Be the negotiation coach; it is your job is to keep everyone energized. Stay positive, and keep them positive. End each session by saying phrases such as, "We've made a lot of progress here today," or "I think we're getting very close now."

- When the negotiation appears to be over, it is not. After the lengthy negotiations on each and every business term in the transaction, attorneys will be engaged to turn the agreements into final language, and they will flesh out everything that is uncertain. As a result of the vagaries of language itself, you will find, once you see a draft of the final documents, that there is a lot more that remains to be negotiated. You thought you had agreed to X but in print, now it looks different. Return to the list of negotiation tips above, and work through the language and get it right.

CONCLUSION

As much as your own ingenuity, talent, and persistence, the terms you negotiate in your early rounds of capital financing will determine the future of your business. A crucial difference is that while your work and vision will shape the business day after day, building up the company in lapidary fashion with layers upon layers of successive progress over the years, the negotiation over your early financing terms, by contrast, happens at a fixed point in time, and then forever after you must live with the confining results of that negotiation. You don't have the luxury to go back and correct the mistakes made in the negotiation. Treat the negotiation phase of your capital raising like a life-and-death matter. In business terms, it is exactly that.

It is also a time of great learning. You will learn valuable relationship lessons about your investors—what really matters to them, how to amicably disagree and move on to find compromise with them. And you will learn as well about what matters most to you. Many of the trade-offs you will be forced to consider in the course of the negotiation will cause you to confront your own belief system and to discover where it is flexible and where it is not. And, of course, you will be acquiring valuable skills that can serve you well in many of life's arenas. Who knows, someday in the future there may come a time when you sense a fight beginning to take its ugly shape with your significant other, and, pausing to take a breath, you'll suddenly say: "You know, it's been a long day, dear, and we've made a lot of progress. Let's take a thirty-minute break, shall we?"

VALUATION MYTH

The common wisdom holds that your initial valuation matters little because you'll make up ground as you grow the business and receive, in return, ever higher valuations in the future. In fact, your initial valuation establishes a gravitational pull that will exert influence on what the market thinks your company is worth long after your first round of funding. No matter how well your business performs between your first and second round of funding, it will not fully escape the force of its initial valuation. When another investor is interested in providing a second round of funding, he or she will go back to look at your previous valuation, and then decide on an appropriate multiple.

The Wire Closes the Deal

Your funding round will close—meaning your round of capital raising will be at a final, irreversible conclusion—when the investor's money arrives in your business checking account. Ka-ching! Until then, however, nothing is certain. The deal is so close . . . but there is still reason to hold your breath. At this point in the process, you have successfully scrambled through all the tortuous terrain in your exotic journey from just another wannabe entrepreneur to Funded Guy. You are exhausted, but look, there it is, you can see the finish line. And with the precious transaction documents now ready to sign, you would think that all that remains is pen and ink, a bank wire, and measuring your head for the correct size of victory crown. This is not what will happen. Ever.

Your deal will never close unless you firmly control the ever-present danger of chaos. At this stage you are going to find yourself in the middle of a classic Three Stooges episode. Everything that can go wrong at this point will. Each time you have readied yourself to receive your well-deserved congratulations, just when you have finished practicing the wonderfully self-deprecating remarks you intend to use to answer the crowd's exultant applause, someone will shove a cream pie in your face. Welcome to closing the deal.

Closing an investment deal is similar to an air traffic controller at LAX trying to organize and manage the incoming approach of a jumbo passenger jet. The plane started its journey in some far-off place, gathered its passengers, successfully took off, traveled hundreds or perhaps thousands of miles through the thin air, and now is circling its final destination. Almost home. Far from its being some routine conclusion to the trip, however, the air traffic controller brings a dizzying array of tools to bear on the all-important task of a safe landing. Without it, everything is lost. Through meticulous management by the air traffic controller, hundreds of potential risks—weather, flocks of errant birds, low-flying amateur pilots out in their two-seater prop planes—have been vetted. Everyone involved in the landing—the pilot of this aircraft, pilots of other aircraft that are taking off or landing, runway personnel—is in constant communication with the controller and knows their responsibilities moment by moment, and, with precise execution, thousands of passengers land safely and on schedule. (OK, not on schedule, but safely.) In an investment transaction, the final landing, the closing, requires the same level of management, except that the air traffic controller is you, the entrepreneur. This secret will prepare you to successfully land your transaction, but be forewarned that strange happenings will find their way into the final moments.

Typical examples that can delay or ruin your deal:

- *Oh, and another thing . . .* Document creep. Investors will want more documentation—"We just remembered we need the so and so opinion in writing as part of the closing documents"—and then when they get this document, they will remember there is some other document that really needs to be produced before the transaction closes.
- *What's your name again?* After the negotiation process has passed, interested parties move on to other deals and lose focus on you. Therefore, you are not getting responses as quickly as you need in order to close on time.
- *The blame game.* Background and due-diligence checks get stranded in limbo, because, according to your investment

partners, they are not getting their own calls returned. They leave messages but have not yet learned that no one will call you back, ever.

- *The empty chair.* One of the investors whose signature you need to finalize the deal goes missing: a sudden bout of malaria, a vacation to the headwaters of the Amazon where there is no means of communication, he broke his signature writing hand in a skiing accident and wants to wait till the cast comes off. You get the idea. I know of a transaction that was set to close, against unchangeable deadlines, on a Monday, but someone whose signature was needed went sailing on the Friday before. The interested parties called around everywhere, but could not track him down. They ended up calling the Coast Guard to locate the sailboat, and got a lawyer out on the bay to apprehend and then board the person's boat on Friday evening, getting the all-important signature before the deal could unravel.

Atypical examples that can delay or ruin your deal:

An earthquake, a bad storm, or a power blackout hits, and the investment firm is temporarily shut down. Or there is a sudden management shake-up at the firm, and nothing is moving forward until the dust settles. Or there is a serious meltdown in the capital markets, and your investors are scrambling to survive their own liquidity squeeze. Not surprisingly, when they are going broke, your investors will not fund your deal, no matter what the contract obliges them to do.

Almost home. You can see the landing strip. Now, how do you get your transaction safely landed?

In order to micromanage the closing and to spite Murphy's Law, assume a seriously obsessive attitude toward details, and follow these five straightforward steps:

STEP 1 Arrange for everyone to agree to the master list of necessary documents in order to close. This organizes the workload of necessary documents and helps to limit document creep.

STEP 2 Create a tick list of who is responsible for producing each item on your master list. Publish this list to all the interested parties, and have everyone sign off on the responsibility list in order to be able to hold each person accountable.

STEP 3 Agree upon an imminent closing date, and drive all necessary closing activities, including the production and signing of documents on your master list, against that date. Convince your investor and the rest of the interested parties to close within one or two weeks: the farther out the date, the more chance you have of people wandering off and getting interested in some other transaction they are working on.

STEP 4 Create a distribution list for everyone who is responsible for any part of the master list. This list should include a directory with each person's e-mail, office phone, cell phone, and home phone. If a person is accountable for a task, you will need to be able to contact them when the inevitable glitch occurs.

STEP 5 Have all principals agree to a preset conference-call schedule. This is an agenda of scheduled conference calls that are needed in order to stay on track and meet the agreed-upon closing date. If the closing is scheduled to conclude in two weeks, arrange to have conference calls twice or three times per week. This is you, the air traffic controller, staying in constant communication with all of the personnel necessary to land the plane safely and on time.

KA-CHING: A NOTE ON WIRING FUNDS

Entrepreneurs who are receiving investment monies for the first time often overlook sending wiring instructions to their investor. As you micromanage the closing, you are going to assign the responsibility of wiring the funds to someone on the investor's team, most likely someone in their accounting department. Create detailed instructions for this person, e-mail the document, and ask for an e-mail confirmation that they received it.

After every item on your master closing list has been accomplished, call and ask the investor's representative if the wire has been sent. When the funds do not arrive on time (they will never arrive on time), do not wait for the investor to figure out why and correct the situation. You have to be active; strange occurrences, acts of God, ghosts of entrepreneurs past roaming the earth, anything can and will get in the way of your closing your deal. Remember, the deal is not closed until the funds show up in your business account.

The honeymoon begins: Once the funds are confirmed and they are secured in your account, call *everyone* involved and congratulate them on a successful closing. Call *everyone* on the copy list and thank them for their efforts, no matter how laborious the closing was and regardless of how inept that particular person was in pitching in to help. Make this an upbeat message. Although we refer to this stage as the "closing," it is really just the beginning of your relationship with your investor. You are now partners with your new investor, and celebrating together is a nice way to begin.

CONCLUSION

Micromanaging the closing, no matter how tedious or frustrating it might prove to be, has its distinct advantages. For one, your deal will close on time. This should be the only motivation you need for losing sleep over every detail of a stressful closing. In micromanaging this final leg of raising start-up capital, you also reinform your investors why they wanted to invest in you in the first place: You know how to make things happen (and make them money in the process). You do not get to be an entrepreneur unless you can conclude this transaction. It is important enough for you to be willing to go a little nuts in tracking every last detail until it's done. You won't have any trouble returning to your easy-going, likable self when the money is in your account.

THE CLOSING MYTH

It is natural to assume that, once everything is completely agreed and only signature signing and paper shuffling remain, the deal will close of its own momentum. This is not how the process plays out. While getting your business funded is one of the most important things in your life at this moment in time, it is likely that this is one of many deals simultaneously under way for your investor. Your investor's attention to closing details will vary depending on many life circumstances over which you have no control. Do not be concerned about this, just get busy. You are the micromanager of the closing. It is up to you to keep everyone working through their responsibilities and land the investment capital in your business account.

Summing Up

Now that you have studied your way through this entire book, you should have a keen appreciation of the difficulties involved in mastering all six secrets of raising start-up capital. It is hard work. In a sense, I believe that it requires such a great deal of work because it is worth it. It is worth it, in the first instance, because raising start-up capital is often the only route to travel in order to see your idea realized in the marketplace. But it is also worth the effort because of the discipline these six steps enforce on you and your management team. You have acquired, in the process, the basic skills of a professional entrepreneur.

These six secrets have caused you to focus, with real intensity, on understanding the key drivers of your business, and they have guided your thinking about recruiting key team members that can match up with those drivers. Through these six secrets, you have learned persuasive methods for articulating the basics of your business concept, even to total strangers. These six secrets have prompted you to research the genuine risks to your business implementation and to do the hard thinking about mitigants to those risks. All of these steps are necessary ingredients to building your business. I often think that there is some kind of cosmic merit system at play, such that if you cannot raise your start-up capital, you are probably not ready to build your business.

There are also side benefits to the process. For instance, you will have learned great discretion in how to spend your company's money. No one knows the value of capital better than the person who is responsible for raising more of it when the money runs out. You will also understand where your business idea and its preparation place you in the wider marketplace of ideas, which is something you cannot learn in the enclosed and somewhat artificial environment of a large corporation.

Do not worry if these steps have seemed awkward during your first time around the capital-raising track. The steps are new to you and require skills that you have yet to become familiar with. Over time, these six secrets will make up the natural rhythm of your business's heartbeat.

Finally, when you check your business account balance, and when, at long last, you can certify that the investor wire has arrived, you should feel justifiably proud. A celebration is in order. Less than 1 percent of those who set out to raise start-up capital are ever successful in raising money. By acquiring investment capital, you have already moved into the upper performance echelons of millions of would-be entrepreneurs. Drink the champagne.

You should be challenged, however, by the realization that, as valuable and rare as your achievement is, it only purchases you a ticket to get onto the playing field. You have arrived, but not in the end zone. You are a newly qualified player now launched into a very fast-moving game.

Once on the field, you will begin to experience all of the ups and downs that attend the building of a business. You will make many mistakes. You will be visited by triumphs and heartaches large and small. You may find being an entrepreneur is everything and more that you dreamed of, or you may find it is not at all what you want for your day-to-day life. You may be delighted by the unfathomable messiness that attends the creative business-building process, or you may find yourself disturbed by the endless chaos. In building your business, all of the correct answers to the really big questions will turn out to be counterintuitive, and this apparent randomness may tickle your need for magical surprise, or it may conflict with your view of intellectual rigor. The start-up experience may make you richer; it may make you poorer. There is nothing inevitable about the future outcome of your life as an entrepreneur. But because you have learned how to raise capital, one thing is certain: you will have a future as an entrepreneur. And you will find out how you match up to the world of your own possibilities. You will know what you and your idea could become. And when you boil it all down, that is the question you wanted to answer, right? *If only.* If only I could raise the capital to take my very own idea out into the world, I wonder what would happen?

It's your turn now. Good luck.

Acknowledgments

Tom Powell was a major contributor to the development of the Six Secrets workshops, providing valuable insight into separate courses geared for entrepreneurs and investors alike. Tom also played a vital role in getting the project of writing the book rolling and maintaining momentum.

Bill West and his company, GhostWest, were instrumental in helping to organize and compile the vast amount of information that formed the basis for this book.

Index

About the Author

BILL FISHER A serial entrepreneur, international seed fund founder, and former executive vice president with Wells Fargo Bank, Bill has been accessing the capital markets to build durable business models for twenty-five years.

Bill managed the Silicon Valley region for Wells Fargo Bank in the 1980s, and in that capacity participated in the meteoric growth of the valley's now famous entrepreneurial culture. He subsequently managed the $12 billion northern California division for Wells, and there he witnessed first-hand the life cycle of thousands of small businesses. His conclusion: timely access to investment capital was the most critical factor to small businesses' long-term success, and too little attention was paid to learning the skills necessary to compete for investment dollars.

Founding his own first business venture in 1995, Fisher began to establish a systematic methodology for efficiently tapping into the capital markets for financing early-stage companies. Since then, his deep understanding of how to speak to the private company investor community has allowed him to raise more than $500 million for a succession of start-up companies.

As a cofounder of the Tiburon family of international seed funds, he has realized twenty-one successful exits, including Xing, Trivago, Cadooz, and Lokalisten.de, along the way successfully coaching scores of entrepreneurs. As founder/cofounder and CEO, he has pioneered new business models with GetSmart.com, GetMobileEurope.de, and Hometown Commercial Capital. As a manager, he has led small, nimble teams and organizations of 15,000 employees. His business-building methods have been featured at Stanford University's Graduate School of Business, and at the World Bank. Soul Htite, cofounder of LendingClub.com, says: "Bill is one of the hidden treasures of Silicon Valley, always willing to share the lessons he's learned with younger entrepreneurs." Bill is an avid fly fisherman, and he resides in northern California with his wife and three children.